BFI FILM CLASSICS

. . . .

Rob White
SERIES EDITOR

Edward Buscombe, Colin MacCabe and David Meeker
SERIES CONSULTANTS

Cinema is a fragile medium. Many of the great films now exist, if at all, in damaged or incomplete prints. Concerned about the deterioration in the physical state of our film heritage, the National Film and Television Archive, part of the British Film Institute's Collections Department, has compiled a list of 360 key works in the history of the cinema. The long-term goal of the Archive is to build a collection of perfect showprints of these films, which will then be screened regularly at the National Film Theatre in London in a year-round repertory.

BFI Film Classics is a series of books intended to introduce, interpret and honour these 360 films. Critics, scholars, novelists and those distinguished in the arts have been invited to write on a film of their choice, drawn from the Archive's list. The numerous illustrations have been made specially from the Archive's own prints.

With new titles published each year, the BFI Film Classics series is a unique, authoritative and highly readable guide to the masterpieces of world cinema.

The best movie publishing idea of the [past] decade.
Philip French, *The Observer*

A remarkable series which does all kinds of varied and divergent things.
Michael Wood, *Sight and Sound*

Exquisitely dimensioned...magnificently concentrated examples of freeform critical poetry.
Uncut

BFI FILM
CLASSICS

THE NIGHT OF THE HUNTER

....

Simon Callow

 Publishing

This book is for Daniel Kramer, another visionary, with love

First published in 2000 by the
BRITISH FILM INSTITUTE
21 Stephen Street, London W1P 2LN

Reprinted 2002

The British Film Institute

promotes greater understanding
and appreciation of, and
access to, film and moving image
culture in the UK.

British Library Cataloguing-in-Publication Data
A catalogue record for this book is available from the British Library

ISBN 0–85170–822–6

Series design by
Andrew Barron & Collis Clements Associates

Typeset in Fournier and Franklin Gothic by
D R Bungay Associates, Burghfield, Berks

Printed in Great Britain by Cromwell Press, Trowbridge, Wiltshire

CONTENTS

INTRODUCTION

Of all the collaborative arts, film is the most complex, owing the most to the greatest number of people, a river into which many streams flow. *The Night of the Hunter* is a supreme example of this confluence. Charles Laughton put his stamp on his first film in a way that it is given to few directors to do. But, as he would have been the first to acknowledge, in the beginning was the word.

In 1953, Davis Grubb, a thirty-five-year-old advertising man from Moundsville, West Virginia, was about to publish his first novel. Paul Gregory, a pushy young manager who had recently started up a company with Laughton, was tipped off that it might be lively material for a film. He was searching for something for Laughton to direct on the screen. As soon as he read the galleys, he knew he was onto a winner. If Laughton had had any doubts about wanting to direct on film, they were dissolved the moment he read *The Night of the Hunter*. He called Grubb as soon as he'd turned the last page and he said to him, 'Man, who are your masters?'

This reaction was of the essence of the man, or perhaps it would be more accurate to say that it was of the essence of the artist. Laughton was

Robert Mitchum, Charles Laughton and Paul Gregory with the book they so faithfully served

that rare thing, an actor who was also an artist. By 1954 he had already given the world a number of indelible creations, performances of such fullness and audacity that they rightfully take their place with creations of other artists, the great writers, the great painters, the great choreographers. He approached his work as a painter might, observing keenly, then submitting his observations to the crucible of his imagination. Transcending mere verisimilitude, the results were more in the way of archetypes – myths through which we can interpret our own reality. To speak of acting in this way makes many people uncomfortable – not least some very good actors – but it is unavoidable in a discussion of Charles Laughton the director, because this is who he was, and this is why his film is what it is. Mindful of the derision with which the utterances of actors are greeted in the Anglo-Saxon countries, Laughton rarely laid his cards on the table; in the mid-50s however he cast caution to the winds and issued the following remarks as part of a publicity hand-out.

> Every actor worth his salt must create the character he plays out of his mind, his perceptions, his experience – otherwise he's not an actor at all. Great acting is like painting. In the great masters of fine art one can see and recognise the small gesture of a finger, the turn of a head, the vitriolic stare, the glazed eye, the pompous mouth, the back bending under a fearful load. In every swerve and stroke of a painter's brush, there is an abundance of life. Great artists reveal the god in man; and every character an actor plays must be this sort of creation. Not imitation – that is merely caricature – and any fool can be a mimic! But creation is a secret. The better – the truer – the creation, the more it will resemble a great painter's immortal work.

Latterly, Laughton had seemed to forsake this ideal in his acting (though it could emerge unannounced at any time), lending his authority and powerful presence to a series of lack-lustre roles it seems he simply could not be bothered to alchemise, as he would say, into creations. Instead, he put his creative energies elsewhere, into his reading tours of America, introducing vast, mainly young, audiences to the idea of the continuity of culture. The readings ranged from the Bible to Plato, Shakespeare to Shaw, ending in a great flourish with the Kerouac of *Dharma Bums*. 'So you see, Ladies and Gentlemen, the Spirit goes *on*!' What he was doing, indirectly, was teaching. And the activity that was closest to his heart at this time was teaching acting. At his house in Curson Avenue in Los Angeles he held classes, sometimes with Charlie Chaplin as guest teacher, for young actors, who formed themselves into the Charles Laughton Players and gave themselves over to his unrelenting probing, challenging and coaching. The idea of craft was central to his work; for months on end, the young American actors, bursting with physical and emotional energy, submitted to what they called the 'de-dum de-dum de-dum' sessions, trying to master the iambic pentameter. In addition, Laughton would expose them to great works of art – many of which he owned himself – asking them to consider what exactly it was that made them extraordinary, both technically and in the whole gesture of the work.

So when Charles Laughton asked Davis Grubb, 'Man, who are your masters?' it was no rhetorical gesture, no colourful praise. He wanted to know.

THE NOVEL

The answer Davis Grubb gave to Laughton was quizzical: Howard Pyle, Hans Christian Andersen, Sax Rohmer. Of these three, Andersen is the most obvious: *The Night of the Hunter* was described by Laughton as 'a sort of Mother Goose tale' which, in an important sense, it is. The influence of the creator of Fu-Manchu is to be felt in Grubb's mastery of suspense and terror. But other influences, unacknowledged, are altogether more present. No American story based on a river journey could escape the example of Mark Twain (notoriously the source, according to Hemingway, of all American literature, though quite where that leaves Melville – who provides two of the epigraphs of Grubb's book – is another matter); nor does *The Night of the Hunter*. Stylistically, there is more than a hint of the Flannery O'Connor of *The Violent Bear It Away* about the writing, and the flow of consciousness can sometimes suggest Faulkner. The cadences of the Bible are everywhere, as well as some fairly heavy fathers of the Church. 'Preacher wouldn't have been possible in a Christian mural, which *The Night of the Hunter* is, in a way,' said Grubb, 'without the influences of St Paul and St Augustine.' Grubb was in the business of making myths, as he tacitly acknowledged in praising Tolkien: 'he is doing so exactly in his time what I want to do in mine.' In terms of the impact of the novel, however – the way in which it works – a more distant influence proves to be the more potent one: that of Charles Dickens, for whom he told Preston Neal Jones he had 'an enormous affinity'.

Grubb's starting point was a story he had toyed with called 'The Gentleman Friend'; before writing *The Night of the Hunter* he had been an occasional contributor to *Collier's Magazine*. In 'The Gentleman Friend', a woman with two children is courted by a salesman, at the same time as a lonely hearts killer is being hunted. An equally potent inspiration for the novel was Grubb's glimpse, in a bar, of a man with 'LOVE' tattooed on one hand and 'HATE' on the other. Grubb had spent some time in Hollywood in his late twenties. 'I was drinking in the local taverns and I got into the habits of the night crawlers and the people who went round at night looking for whatever: loneliness, or drugs, or sex. A lot of that', he said, 'later went into *The Night of the Hunter*, in a funny way.'

Grubb was a sophisticated man (as his own list of references would suggest: the living writer he most admired was Rebecca West). He grew up on the banks of the Ohio river, and was profoundly imbued with its sounds and smells and savours; but he came from a reasonably well-heeled background. His father was an architect ('in Wheeling, a great man') who died when he was young; his mother was always saving kids in trouble. In time she became a social worker. He formed a belief in the overpowering importance of women:

> women held this country together during the pioneer days, and I think they held it together during the depression. I don't think this country ever would have made it without women … when women have linked hands and saved the country … I saw the pride of men who had been strong, self-sustaining people, taking care of their families. I saw that broken. And the reaction to that, in most men, is a terrible social anger. And I've seen the women appease that, and probably save us from great violence.

There is nothing *faux-naif* about Grubb's writing; he deliberately chose to tell his story as an allegory of the struggle between good and evil: a Christian mural, as he says, in which the Preacher has the part of the devil. The novel has a five-part structure, with an overall epigraph from *Moby-Dick*: 'Where do murderers go, man? Who's to doom when the judge himself is dragged to the bar?' Each section has its own epigraph: 'The Hanging Man' from Donne – 'Wilt thou forgive that sinne by which I'have wonne/ Others to sinne? And, made my sinne their door?'; 'The Hunter', a child's rhyme – 'Run, puppy, run! Run, puppy, run! Yonder comes the big dog, run, puppy, run!'; 'The River' from Kipling – 'Not cleverness, child, but only thought. A little thought in life is like salt upon rice, as the boatmen say …'; and Melville again for 'A Strong Tree with

Many Birds' – 'Oh, the gold! The precious, precious gold! The green miser'll horde ye soon! Hish! Hish! God goes 'mong the worlds blackberrying!' The Epilogue, 'They Abide' is prefaced with a quote from Hopkins: 'I say that we are wound/ With mercy round and round/ As if with air!'

It is perhaps worth observing here that the book is not best served by short quotations: Grubb's achievement is to have created by rhythm and tone a cumulative flow which carries the reader through in one arc from the beginning to the very end; the book was completed in six weeks. Nonetheless, the vivid, etched visual element – almost as if in cut-out form – is immediately apparent, as well as the swiftly moving succession of scenes. No wonder Paul Gregory leaped at it; the word that comes unbidden to mind is *cinematic*. 'I had been filming *The Night of the Hunter* in my head as I wrote it,' he told Preston Neal Jones. Grubb binds his first section ('The Hanging Man') with the refrain of the children's mocking rhyme ('Hing, Hang, Hung! Hung, Hang, Hing!') which John forbids his uncomprehending sister to sing; that too translates directly to the screen. Dialogue is rendered without inverted commas, to facilitate the flow. We are often taken inside the protagonists' heads – especially John's, as he tries to resolve the contradictions of his world, which is both any child's world (tiresome younger sisters), and that of one particular hapless child, haunted by the memory of watching his father taken away by 'the blue men', with their sticks and guns, and struggling to deal with the new order ushered in by his loss. Other characters in the book are allotted these inner ruminations, too; in the final section of the book they become fully fledged streams-of-consciousness. In the nature of things, this is the hardest of the book's devices to absorb into the film.

The tone of the book is established in the first paragraph:

A child's hand and a piece of chalk had made it: a careful, child's scrawl of white lines on the red bricks of the wall beside Jander's Livery Stable: a crude pair of sticks for the gallows tree, a thick broken line for the rope, and then the scarecrow of the hanging man. Some passing by along that road did not see it at all; others saw it and remembered what it meant and thought solemn thoughts and turned their eyes to the house down the river road. The little children – the poor little children. Theirs were the eyes for which the crude picture was intended and they had seen it and heard along Peacock Alley the mocking child rhyme that went with it. And now, in the kitchen of that stricken house, they ate their breakfast in silence.

The story of the novel is simply told. It is the depressed 30s in Ohio. Ben Harper has shot and killed two men in a stick-up at a gas station. He is sentenced to hang. While in prison, Ben shares a cell with an itinerant preacher, Harry Powell, arrested for stealing a car. Unbeknown to the authorities, he has a history of killing rich widows; the letters L, O, V, E and H, A, T, E are spelled out on the fingers of either hand. Powell tries to prise out of Ben the secret of where he has hidden the money from his crime; but Ben gives nothing away. Preacher's interrogation of Ben Harper in the jail is typical of Grubb's way with dialogue, and indeed found its way directly into the film:

> Now Preacher comes back and stands by Ben's bunk.
> Set your soul right, Ben Harper! That money's bloodied with Satan's own curse now. And the only way it can get cleared of it is to let it do His works in the hands of good, honest poor folks.
> Like you, Preacher?
> I am a man of Salvation!
> You, Preacher?
> I serve the Lord in my humble way, Ben.
> Then, says Ben Harper softly, how come they got you locked up in Moundsville Penitentiary, Preacher?
> There are those that serves Satan's purposes against the Lord's servants, Ben Harper.
> And how come you got that stick knife hid in your bed blankets, Preacher?
> I serve God and I come not with peace but with a sword! God blinded mine enemies when they brought me to this evil place and I smuggled it in right under the noses of them damned guards. That sword has served me through many an evil time, Ben Harper.
> I'll bet it has, Preacher, grins Ben ...

Soon enough, he is hanged. The narrative spine of the first section is driven by a single question: where is the money? Where has Ben hidden it? Where? The only person who knows is John. 'It was not a knowing that he could share with his mother or with anyone. It was a secret that was a little world of its own. A terrible little world like an island upon whose haunted beach he wandered alone now, like a solitary and stricken Crusoe, while everywhere about him his eyes would find the footprint of the dangling man.' At the book's opening Willa is travelling to the penitentiary to ask Ben that very question. After she leaves, Ben recalls

Willa's visit, speaking to him only of the money: 'until her face began to look for all the world like the face of Preacher; weak and sick with greed; the same greed that had led Ben to murder and the gallows.' He recalls the trial: even the court wants to know where the money is. They offer to commute his sentence if only he'll tell them, but he prefers the grim satisfaction of going to the grave with his secret. In sleep, he murmurs out loud, quoting the Bible: 'and a little child shall lead them.'

Preacher too drifts into dreams: dwelling on the women he has killed. He could never be exactly sure how many there had been. Sometimes there were twelve and sometimes it was only six 'and then again they would all blend together into one and her face would rise up in the wavering chiaroscuro of his dreams like the Whore of Sodom and not until his hand stole under his blanket and wound round the bone hasp of the faithful knife did the face blanch and dissolve into a spasm of horror and flee back into the darkness again'. Grubb graphically depicts Powell's psychopathic progress, as, driven by inner whisperings, he cuts a murderous swathe through the gullible widows of the land. Now he is obsessed by something else. Even as Ben is taken to be hanged Preacher screams his question after him: *'where's the money?'* After the hanging, the hangman and a crony discuss the hanged man. 'I figure he was a feller that wasn't used to killin' – a good sort at heart, what I mean to say.' Even they wonder where the money is. The hangman goes home; he's weary of his frightful occupation. He wants to go back to work in the mines. His wife forbids him; she needs him alive. He gazes fondly at his own two children.

Back at Cresap's Landing, Willa has taken a job at the ice-cream parlour run by Walt and Icey Spoon. Grubb depicts the community with a sharp and sometimes fanciful touch: the Spoons – kindly Walt and garrulous, match-making Icey (named for her skill in the ice-cream department) – and the bizarre Miz Cunningham, in whose pawn shop John spots the watch that he longs for beyond anything else in the world. Miz Cunningham as described by Grubb would not have disdained the company of Mrs Gamp:

> Why, she was really quite wonderful – this old fat woman! In the end, she got her hands on nearly everything in the world! Just look at her window! There by the pair of old overshoes were Jamey Hankins' ice-skates! There was old Walt Spoon's elk's tooth. There – his mother's own wedding ring! There was a world in that window of this remarkable old woman. And it was probable that when Miz

Cunningham like an ancient barn owl fluttered and flapped to earth at last, they would take her away and pluck her open and find her belly lined with fur and feathers and the tiny mice skulls of myriad dreams.

She wants to know about the money too, of course.

Back in the ice-cream parlour, Icey is urging Willa to remarry, and consults the Ouija board as to her potential husband. The word 'CLOTH' is spelt out. On cue, Preacher, now discharged from prison, arrives, by means of a *coup de théâtre*, which, like so much else in the book, translates directly into film. There is a gas lamp outside Willa's house. 'And when the wind tossed the branches of the tree the light from the gas lamp made pictures on the wall of the children's bedroom. The twisted, barren winter branches tossed stiffly in the golden light and yet with a curious grace, like the fingers of old men spinning tales ...' Using his hands to create a shadow play, John summons up a horse prancing, a soldier, a clown. His own shadow looms up menacingly, which he quells with his toy pistol, running back to bed. But when he looks up, the shadow man is still there: 'a very silent, motionless man with a narrow-brimmed hat and still, straight arms ... then he saw the man by the roadside ... staring speculatively toward the house like a traveler seeking a night's lodging. Go away, man! Whispered John, his flesh gathering for a paroxysm of trembling.' John sneaks a proscribed visit to his only friend, Uncle Birdie Steptoe, the alcoholic fisherman; another Dickensian figure, who tells John that Preacher is a friend of his father's from prison. Troubled, John heads for the ice-cream parlour, finding his mother and Pearl and the Spoons mesmerised by the Preacher as he performs his 'parable of Right-Hand-Left-Hand, the struggle between LOVE and HATE'. John alone resists his charms. His mother, particularly taken, is furious at John's resistance. 'Willa's breath stirred in his ear, hot and furious, choking with humiliation. "You just wait, John Harper! Just wait till I git you home!"'

The screw tightens in the second section, 'The Hunter'. Preacher stays on at Cresap's Landing, and starts courting Willa. She confides in Icey that Preacher has told her that Ben threw the money in the Ohio river. They all go on a church picnic at the old graveyard upriver, where Ben is buried. John is terrified of having to speak to Preacher, but he speaks first: '"John, I don't believe you like me very much." He could not make the lie with his mouth so he sat mute and blushing.' They travel back through a storm. Preacher leads the singing of hymns, but John cannot sing. Preacher grips his shoulders.

Why aren't you singin', boy? Trying now to make the harbour! In the darkness may be lost! The fingers were tightening, like the steel pincers of a tool, in the soft flesh of the boy's shoulder. He tried to wrench free but the grip went under the tendons, around the shoulder bone. – Sing, boy! Sing! Came the hot and furious whisper in his eyes. Goddam you, sing the hymn! – I don't know no words! John cried out suddenly and the fingers sprang free. I don't know no words!

It is spring. 'If, in this urgent season of mating, Willa found the attentions of Preacher attractive and exciting, to Icey Spoon they were a challenging imperative.' Willa feels no desire for the Preacher, not what she felt for Ben. 'Fiddlesticks! That wasn't love, honey. That was just hot britches. There's more to a marriage than four bare legs in a bed. When you're married forty years you'll know that all that don't matter a hill of beans. I been married that long to my Walt now and I'll swear in all that time whenever he took me, I'd just lie there thinking about my canning …' – another piece of dialogue which finds its way directly into the film. Preacher proposes to Willa, and despite a dark premonition – 'she did not know herself whose voice this was, deep in the vast river murmurs of her mind, that kept telling her not to do this thing' – she accepts. John returns home, to find that Preacher is there. In a scene reminiscent of *David Copperfield*, it is Preacher and not Willa who breaks the news of the coming marriage to John. 'You ain't my dad! breathed John. You won't never be my dad! He was not scared anymore; his anger swung and blazed in the dark room like a pine torch.' Then, fatally, he cries (of the money): 'You think you can make me tell! He had screamed, till the house was shrill with it. But I won't! I won't! I won't!' Now the hunt is on in earnest.

Preacher and Willa marry, while the children stay overnight with Icey. Willa's wedding night is a harsh shock to her. Preacher shames her for even entertaining the notion of consummation, forcing her to stand naked and shivering in front of the mirror. John darkly notes the change that overcomes his mother after the wedding. 'Her eyes bore dark shadows and her mouth was thinner – paler – and her flesh itself seemed to have capitulated to the urgent moral protocols of her marriage until the very roundness of her sweet figure had turned epicene and sour in that lean season.' Willa makes public renunciation of the flesh, and, at a revivalist meeting, proclaims that Ben Harper threw the money in the river. In fact, we now discover for the first time, the money is in Pearl's rag doll. One evening she opens up the doll, tipping out the pretty hundred dollar bills to play with them, cutting them up and letting them blow away in the wind.

John saves the day in the nick of time; finally the kids go to bed and John dreams about the day of his father's arrest, and the frantic decision to put the money in the doll, and the solemn injunction which he lays on John. And it is only now, at this point in the novel, and in John's dream, that we are told the full story. There follows a dream of Willa's, of her wedding night with Ben, in all its boozy sensuality, and Ben's desperate resolve, even then, that 'I'll never let a kid of mine want. It don't matter how I git it – no youngin of mine will ever want for nothin' '. Then, in another highly cinematic moment, we shift to another bedroom, that of Icey and Walt Spoon. Walt has his doubts about the Preacher; Icey dispels them. 'It was something he had learned to do in their marriage: hammering his thoughts into the shape she wanted ... it's true, he thought. He's a Man of God. Yes, anyone can tell that.'

The book's third section, 'The River', begins with John and Uncle Birdie fishing for gar (needlefish, sharp-toothed and long-jawed).

> John's eyes peered into the water until they ached, and ... every cloud or bird that passed above them in the afternoon cast its image in the mirroring river and seemed to the boy to be the black hunter ... Like him. Like his ways. Sneaking around after the bait, only he ain't as smart as a gar – he don't know where the bait is so he can't steal it.

Back at home, Willa overhears the Preacher's violent rage against Pearl: 'His voice was as swift and solid in the evening silence as the thump of a butcher's cleaver in the block. "*Where's the money?* Tell me, you little bitch, or I'll tear your arm off!"' Willa comforts Pearl, then repairs to bed, where Preacher interrogates her yet again about the money. She falls into a dream-like state.

> Then she thought: Why is my lip bleeding? Why can I taste the blood running back into my teeth and tongue? And then she remembered that he had struck her with the dry, shiny flat of his hand and it had happened only a second before though it seemed like a long time ... and the dark gar wheeled patiently in his pool again, the long sentry of circling dusk and shadow, of wisdom and darkness under the sun-dappled pool. He had risen from the bed now and stood silhouetted against the square of moonlit window and his head was cocked a little toward the light as if harking to a whisper late in coming, and she thought: Why, he is so little. He is only a child. He looks like a little boy in his nightshirt. It was Ben who was the grown-up, dirty man.

Willa tells him she knows that the money was no part of his reason for marrying her: he came to save her. 'But he did not hear because now the night was filled with Whispers and they were for him. And she knew suddenly that he was not going to ever say anything more to her as long as she lived; that whatever was going to happen next would be not words but a doing. But still she kept on.' She knows that she must suffer more: 'Praise God! She cried as he pulled down the window blind and the pagan moon was gone and something clicked and switched softly open and she heard the swift rushing whisper of his bare feet on the floor as he moved through the darkness toward the bed and she thought: It is some kind of razor he shaves with. I knowed what it was the first night.'

We then cut (the terminology is inevitable) to John hearing the car being started up in the middle of the night. Cut again to the Spoons with the news of Willa's alleged decampment: Preacher is heart-broken. After receiving their consolations, he returns to the house to pursue his interrogation of the children, who hide in the cellar. Preacher forces them out. Uncle Birdie meanwhile has discovered Willa's body in the river. He tells his dead wife about it. "Twas there I seen it, Bess. Down there in all that water. Ben Harper's old Model T and her in it! … just a-sittin' there in a white gown and her eyes looking at me and a great long slit under her chin just as clean as a catfish gill! … and her hair wavin' lazy and soft around her like meadow grass under flood waters …' an image which provided Laughton with one of the most haunting sequences in the film. John, meanwhile, lures Preacher back down into the cellar again: 'John slammed the door behind him with all his might. Preacher screamed in anguish and John felt the evil fingers crush between the door and the jamb … and slammed again and pushed the door tight and before Preacher could rally the iron bolt flew home.'

The children's flight commences. They are pursued by Preacher's cries, entreating at first, then violent: 'ANSWER ME, YOU SPAWN OF THE DEVIL'S OWN WHORE!' They head for the river. 'That is the only where. The warm, dark mother river running in the summer night and the only friend in the whole, swarming, vast and terrible darkness.' John finds Ben's old skiff and by a superhuman effort he manages to push the boat into the middle of the river leaving Preacher stranded up to his waist in water. 'They could see the livid, twisted, raging oval of his face: the mouth gaping and sick with hatred … and now some errant current in the vast, dark river caught them upon its warm wing and the boat began moving, blessedly moving, spinning at first like a mad October leaf and then heading into the channel while they could still hear Preacher … he began a

steady, rhythmical animal scream of outrage and loss.' But natural healing
is at hand. 'Those river folk fell silent, waiting for it to stop, waiting for the
flowing river night to wash it into the darkness again and leave the hour to
the sounds a night should have: the scritch of green frogs, the sudden leap-
ing of a fish, the squeal of a buck hare up in the orchard before the ravening
weasel's leap.' It will be seen how, again and again, Laughton and his collaborators directly translate Grubb's text into film.

> To have seen the children in that troubled time one might have supposed
> them to be fallen angels, or dusty woodland elves suddenly banished
> from the Court of the Gods of Moonlight and of faery meadows. They
> blew along like brown leaves on the wind. All the long hot day after their
> escape they had drifted upon the swift river channel and then the river
> night dropped abruptly upon them and there were no lights but the stars
> and the shantyboat lamps along the shore and the drifting dust of fireflies
> against the black, looming hills above the narrows.

They scavenge for food, but they are not alone in their foraging: 'It was
no strange sight in the land in that lean and fallow time: children running
the woodlands and the fields without parents, without food, without
love.' The times are savage: 'Go away! The fat woman's eyes seemed to
say. Go away because you remind me of something dreadful in the land
just now: some pattern that is breaking up: something going on that is as
basic and old as the wheeling of winter stars. Go away! Don't remind me
that it's Hard Times and there's children on the roads of the land!'

The threat of Preacher is never far away, either, as he doggedly
makes his way towards them. John finds them a barn to sleep in, but
awakens to a familiar sound: 'As plain and clear as the song of the now-
stilled field bird had been he had heard the faint, sweet rise of that
unforgettable voice. Leaning, leaning! Safe and secure from all alarms!
Leaning, leaning! Leaning on the everlasting arms.' Mercifully, he passes
by. 'John could still hear the faint, sweet voice and he thought: Don't he
never sleep?' And so the children's flight continues.

As in all the best fables, help, finally, arrives, in initially unpromising
form. 'I'll fetch a willow switch and bring you up here *jumpin'* directly! ...
the woman was in her middle-sixties, staunch and ruddy-faced and big-
boned. She wore a man's old hat on her head and a shapeless gray wool
sweater hung over her shoulders. Now she snorted like a fieldhand.' This is
Rachel Cooper, and she takes the children firmly in hand, starting by clean-
ing them up. 'John shivered at the prospect. And yet his heart was curiously

warm within him with the unreasonable illusion that he had come home.' So ends 'The River' section of *The Night of the Hunter*. Dickens's Betsy Trotwood would have recognised a kindred spirit in Rachel Cooper.

Her establishment gives its name to the section – 'A Strong Tree with Many Birds'. It consists of three abandoned children, Clara, Mary and Ruby, the problem child, clumsy but kind. Ruby takes charge of Pearl; and Rachel makes it her special task to draw John into the charmed circle of her affections, reading to the children from scripture. He is mesmerised by the story of Moses and sees himself and Pearl as two tiny floating kings: 'I am a lost King and Pearl is a lost King too.' Ruby, sent by Rachel into the nearby town of New Economy to learn sewing, has discovered sex instead: 'she had found a wonderful thing that she could do well.' Preacher by chance finds Ruby and charms her and bribes her with the gift of a movie magazine into telling him about the children, and then the nightmare begins all over again. Rachel finds the magazine; Ruby confesses all, and describes Preacher. A day later, he arrives to collect the children. Rachel instantly sees through him. 'The years alone in the nights of river silence and river wind had taught her the wisdom of stable beasts; the cunnings of the small creatures of the woods.'

When he tries to reclaim John against his will she confronts Preacher: 'Old Rachel loomed above him then in the stone threshold … the blue barrel of the pump gun was steady as doom in her old hands … Preacher, on all fours beneath the puzzle tree, lifted his face slowly to the gun muzzle and then to Rachel's face. His features were yellow with it now: the raging uncontrollable fury.' He goes, returning that night to lay siege to the house. He sits on a locust stump; Rachel sits vigil in her window. She gathers the children around her, telling them the tale of the Massacre of the Innocents, then sends them away. Preacher pounces. 'He rocketed suddenly upward before her very eyes, his twisted mask caught for one split second in the silver moonlight like the vision in a photograph negative and she saw the knife in his fist rise swiftly as the bobbin of a sewing machine just as she began pulling the trigger while the gun bucked and boomed in her hands.' Rachel calls for the State Troopers to come and arrest Preacher who, his arm shattered by Rachel's bullets, has been hiding in her barn. When the Troopers – the men in blue – arrive, John is horribly reminded of an earlier arrest. He rushes forward with the doll. 'Here! Here! he screamed, flogging the man in the grass with the limp doll until his arms ached. Here! Take it back! I can't stand it, Dad! It's too much, Dad! I can't stand it! Here! I don't want it! I don't want it! It's too much! I can't do it! Here! Here!'

Preacher is taken away; John is gently put to bed. There follows a long and striking interior monologue of John's. He no longer remembers any of what has happened to him, nor even who Preacher is. In court, he has been unable to testify. 'They keep asking me to remember all kinds of stuff. The thing they don't know is that it was a dream and when you tell about a dream it is not all there the way they want it to be.' Icey and Walt Spoon have come to town for the trial; Icey has been screaming and ranting against Preacher in the courtroom. John doesn't know who she is. She spots him and Pearl in a café and points them out to the crowd, but John has no idea why. In the courtroom, the prosecutor indicates Preacher but John refuses to look at him; all this is described in John's inner monologue. The novel then switches to an equivalent monologue for Ruby, who is still sweet on Preacher. 'Well, he don't make fun of me and laugh at me like them boys used to do and he don't want to do the dirty thing.' She becomes aware of a mob heading for the courthouse and believes that they're bent on freeing Preacher. She goes to help them, but they pack her off. She goes back to Rachel Cooper's, while Walt is screaming at the mob as they descend on Preacher. 'Because he tricked us! Because he tricked us.'

The final section of the novel, the Epilogue, is entitled 'They Abide', an allusion to Rachel's observation the morning after Preacher has been wounded: 'children are man at his strongest, that they are possessed, in those few short seasons of the little years, of more strength and endurance than God is ever to grant them again. They abide.' It is Christmas time. 'Rachel reflected about children. One would think the world might be ashamed to name such a day for one of them and go on the same old way.' All children need protection:

> because with every child ever born of woman's womb, there is a time of running through a shadowed place, an alley with no doors, and a hunter whose footsteps ring brightly along the bricks behind him. With every child – rich or poor – however favoured, however warm and safe in the nursery, there is this time of echoing and vast aloneness, when there is no one to come nor to hear, and dry leaves scurrying past along a street become the rustle of Dread and the ticking of the old house is the cocking of the hunter's gun. For even when the older ones love and care and are troubled for the small ones there is little they can do as they look into the grave and stricken eyes that are windows to this affrighted nursery province beyond all succour, all comforting.

She reads them the Christmas story, then they give each other presents. John gives Rachel an apple, she gives him a watch. 'It sure will be nice to have someone around the house who can give me the right time of day!' John recalls the Christmas story and, noting that Mary and Joseph were put up in a barn, looks out at Rachel's barn: no sign of them. 'You never know what they tell you. You never find out if it's real or a story ... I wish I could remember stuff. It all gets mixed up inside you. And sometimes you can't remember if things is real or just a story. You never know.' With his new watch he goes to bed. As in the old days, he studies the shadows on the wall, then gets out and makes one of his own. He whispers to the shadows: 'I ain't afraid of you! ... I got a watch that ticks! I got a watch that shines in the dark!' Going back to bed he waits to see if he has somehow conjured up the bogey-man again. But no.

> The night of the hunter was gone forever and the blue men would not come again. And so John pulled the gospel quilt snug around his ear and fell into a dreamless winter sleep, curled up beneath the quaint, stiff calico figures of the world's forgotten kings, and the strong, gentle shepherds of that fallen, ancient time who had guarded their small lambs against the night.

The book becomes more and more John's as it progresses; by the end, we understand that we have been reading his story.

It has seemed valuable to give a detailed impression of the novel to give an indication of how closely the film follows it, and to see why it diverges when it does. This is the book Laughton fell in love with; he remained in love with it, and his every effort was dedicated to realising it on screen as best he could, in as much detail as possible. This seemingly obvious approach is worth stressing because it is far from automatic. It would not be an exaggeration to say that film-makers are generally concerned to make their source material serve the film, rather than have the film serve the source material. In this, as in much else, Laughton was out of the ordinary.

THE SCREENPLAY

It was highly unusual, for example, for a film-maker to seek as actively as Laughton did to involve the original author in the film. To Laughton it was the obvious thing to do. He and Gregory had agreed that it would be unwise for Laughton to attempt to write the screenplay himself. An experienced screenwriter was needed. In the event, they chose one of the highest high-flyers of his day, James Agee, poet, novelist, film critic and scenarist of *The African Queen*, which he had written ten years before for John Huston. Some ten years older than Davis Grubb, his background was not dissimilar – he came from Knoxville, in Tennessee – and he had written, in *Let Us Now Praise Famous Men*, the definitive evocation of the rural Depression of the 30s, exactly the milieu of *The Night of the Hunter*. But although Grubb's novel, as we have seen, engages with the period – and indeed the mainspring of the plot, Ben Harper's crime, might be said to be a direct by-product of the Depression – its focus is very much more on a child's rites of passage, the conquest of his demons of anxiety and doubt.

Here too, though, Agee was an inspired choice. He had recently resolved to concentrate exclusively on his family background in his own writing, particularly his childhood: 'Now as awareness of how much of life is lost, and how little is left, becomes even more piercing, I feel also, and ever the more urgently, the desire to restore, and to make a little less impermanent, such of my lost life as I can, beginning with the beginning and coming as far forward as need be. This is the simplest, most primitive of the desires which can move a writer.' The work he was engaged on around the time that he was working on *The Night of the Hunter* was the book that would prove to be his swansong, the posthumously published novel *A Death in the Family*, whose famous opening, 'Knoxville: Summer 1915', enters into the child's-world view with profound sympathy. But Rufus, Agee's autobiographically based child-hero, is a far cry from Grubb's unhappy John. 'All my people are larger bodies than mine, quiet, with voices gentle and meaningless like the voices of sleeping birds … one is my mother who is good to me. One is my father who is good to me. By some chance, here they are, all on this earth.' This is day to *The Night of the Hunter*'s night; but there can be no doubt of Agee's emotional and intellectual sympathy with Grubb's novel. He was hired for the substantial sum – in 1954 – of $30,000 and set to work.

It can scarcely have been unknown to Gregory, a shrewd and unsentimental operator, that Agee, genial and gifted man that he was, was also drinking himself in short order into an early grave; a younger contemporary noted him as a 'whiskey-listless and excessive saint'. No doubt it was worth the gamble; a great deal of very remarkable work has been produced down the centuries by alcoholics, and no doubt Gregory and Laughton believed they could contain his excesses; his name on the poster was alone worth the effort. Clearly, from Gregory's report, things went horribly wrong very soon. He describes Agee as lying, incapable, on the floor of his – Gregory's – guest house in Santa Monica for fourteen days, after which they moved him into the Chateau Marmont. 'Charles wouldn't come near him … and because of that Jim drank even more.' Nonetheless, he managed to produce a 350-page script, which, says Gregory, 'Charles never opened'. This script has disappeared. Agee's biographer says this of it: 'he had re-created a cinematic version of [the novel] in great detail. He specified use of newsreel footage to document the story's setting and added any number of elaborate, impractical montages.' The truth is that Agee, for all his undoubted brilliance as a critic, had only ever written two screenplays that had reached the screen, and one of those was 'adapted for the screen by James Agee and John Huston'. He was not exactly what one might call a hardy professional at the craft. Clearly, as the starting date of shooting began to loom ominously, swift action had to be taken, and Laughton took it. Agee remained with the movie just long enough for Laughton 'to have a vision and some inspiration to write his own script … out of the terrible disagreements with Agee'. This is Gregory's report.

It is important at this point to enter a caveat about Gregory's testimony. Yet another complex man, he had axes of many kinds to grind, although his evidence, as originator and highly active producer of the film, should by no means be discounted. His principal concern over the years that followed his split from Charles Laughton was to make sense of their relationship, both for himself and for the outside world, which led him into many extreme statements, expressed with striking vividness. It was important in his personal mythology that Laughton should be seen to be a monster nonetheless capable, if properly handled, of greatness. He thus claimed that Agee's problems were exacerbated, if not actually created, by Laughton and that the relationship was bound to have been catastrophic because Laughton had been so harsh to Gregory himself.

This account is somewhat contradicted by the meagre evidence that we have. There is a very civil and practical memo from Laughton to Agee, for example, dated 16 July 1954, a couple of months before shooting began, making a detailed suggestion about the shot in which Rachel reads the story of Pharaoh to the children: a certain sequence of shots, Laughton proposes, will avoid any interference by the Breen office. 'If we make it very clear that we are for religion, and not against it in this passage, we shall have an easier time with them.' He also proposes reversing the order of words in a line. These are scarcely the communications of a director who has abandoned his screenwriter. There is a memo from Agee to Laughton regretting his absence for a week or two while he discharges another writing commitment. And finally, most revealingly, there is a long letter from Agee dated January 1955, a couple of months after shooting was completed, concerning something that obviously exercised him deeply: the matter of the credit. In the history of writer/director relationships, it is a most unusual letter because it argues for a *smaller* credit than the one contracted. 'My feeling was, and is,' writes Agee,

> that Charles had such an immense amount to do with the script, that it seems to me absurd to take solo credit, much as I'd like it … I'm sure you know as well as I do or better, how embarrassed a writer should rightly feel in being given full credit, who has done a piece of work for and with Charles. It's on this basis that I feel very strongly that credit on the script should be double. At times, I've even felt that it should be given to him entirely; I can withdraw from that position only in realising that I was useful, as a sort of combination sounding-board and counterirritant.

Clearly the matter had been mooted before, because Agee says 'Charles's own feeling … fell into 2 parts: 1) he doesn't like the idea of being talked about as a "genius" or a credit-hog, as he felt might happen if we split credit 2) realising how intricate the collaboration is, in actual practice, in crystallising any kind of show, he felt strongly that the front, the thing presented to the world, should remain ultra-simple and clear.' These two eminently practical considerations were evidently accepted by all the concerned parties. (The first point reads like a reference to the widely reported *Citizen Kane* controversy, when the Screen Writers' Guild had to do battle on behalf of Herman J. Mankiewicz to secure him even half a credit.) Agee was too genuinely modest to acknowledge that his own name constituted a source of lustre, but his comments make clear without any doubt the huge input that Laughton had at every level.

It is also, incidentally, not the letter of a destroyed alcoholic, whatever boozy interludes may intermittently have occurred, nor that of someone who had been treated abominably by Laughton and kicked off the film, nor indeed that of someone who felt he had no connection with the movie as it had been shot. 'Needless to say,' he adds, 'I am deeply eager to see the film at whatever stage it's see-able.' Gregory wrote back:

We do not feel, in any sense, that a change on the credit should be made where you are concerned. We feel that you made a great contribution to *The Night of the Hunter*. I tell you very honestly if we thought the picture were bad, in order to protect you, we would be more than happy to remove your name, but since we think it is great, we feel that you will be happy and proud that you had something to do with it – and neither Charles nor I feel that under any circumstances you should be embarrassed over the credit.

The relationship remained cordial to the end. When Agee died, in May 1955, four months before the release of the film, Laughton sent a telegram to Mrs Agee: 'Just heard sad news of James passing. I loved him.'

What then, was the nature of Laughton's contribution to the screenplay? It is worth noting that he had come to *The Night of the Hunter* on the back of a string of directorial successes in the theatre, all produced by, and to some extent suggested by, Paul Gregory, and all largely dependent on Laughton's skill as an editor of texts. The scripts of *Don Juan in Hell*, Stephen Vincent Benét's *John Brown's Body* and most recently *The Caine Mutiny Court Martial* were all subjected to his cutting and reshaping, above all the last, on which he was still working while preparing the screenplay for *The Night of the Hunter*. Charles Nolte, who played Keith in the production, has, in a remarkable unpublished rehearsal journal, 'The Caine Rehearsals', described the absolute ruthlessness with which Laughton shaped the material, paring down, stripping away excess. Some of this skill he had learned while collaborating with Bertolt Brecht on *Galileo* in 1947; they shared a taste for Japanese art with its clean, clear lines, and both saw the theatre and film as essentially educative. Timid and even cowardly in life, Laughton pulled no punches when it came to art, and many people have testified to the almost annihilating force which he would bring to the matter in hand, whether it was writing or acting. He was, after all, Charles Laughton, on whose tyrants and monsters over the previous twenty years all his collaborators had been raised. It may indeed have proved alarming for Agee to be subjected to this process, but, as his letter proves, he was glad of it in the end.

The first question Laughton must have asked concerned the nature of the material, or, to put it more crudely, what was the novel *about*? One of the things that it was about was very clear to Laughton from the beginning. 'Hollywood has been looking for forty years, Davis,' he told Grubb, 'to find a story about the church, what it is and what it does, and you've found a way of doing it that we can put over.' Laughton certainly had feelings about religion. Brought up as a strict Roman Catholic, he had been sent to the Jesuit college of Stonyhurst, which he left early under something of a cloud. In the memoirs he was fitfully dictating to Bruce Zortman on his deathbed, he describes some sort of incident that involved self-exposure during a religious service, a connection between the erotic and the ecclesiastical that was ruthlessly punished, and which caused deep distress to his family, thus only confirming his sense of himself as some sort of pariah. Ejection from Stonyhurst was the beginning of the end for his commitment to the Catholic Church, or any church. He told Grubb that during the First World War, in the last year of which he fought, a padre had come round his battalion in the trenches, to give them absolution. Laughton said to him, 'No thanks, Father, I think I can take it from here alone.' Gregory saw Laughton's loathing of religion as central to his attraction to the novel, but in a complex way. He expresses himself characteristically colourfully: 'There was much that was saintly in Charles Laughton. And with the young children aspect of it, and the devil in Preacher Powell that gave Laughton both heaven and hell to play with. He was the master of both of those at the time. The man was a saint/sinner. I think that was his nature, like an alligator is an alligator. He was anti-religious, absolutely anti-religious in the denominational sense and I think that it was a marvellous opportunity to show that God's glory was really in the little old farm woman, and not in the Bible totin' sonofabitch.'

Gregory himself had an intensely personal response to the book. He claimed in an interview that he wanted to film *The Night of the Hunter* to allow as many people as possible 'to share the warm feeling of hope I received from this haunting novel'. He was, he later said, drawn to it because 'it paralleled emotionally ... aspects of my life. The little children that are deserted'. Born Jason Lenhart, he had been abandoned by his father, changed his name, and forged a career of some distinction. Many years later, the man had turned up at a festival in Gregory's honour, knocked on his hotel door, and asked to see Jason Lenhart. 'He's not here,' said Gregory, closed the door, and threw up. He never saw him again.

Laughton's own relationship to childhood and fatherhood was, like everything else about him, complex. Highly conscious of his unorthodox appearance (in adulthood he would say 'I have the face of a departing pachyderm') and wrestling furiously with a strong sexual appetite, strongly focused on his own sex, he had a turbulent childhood, one whose repressions and concealments were nonetheless balanced by intense early experience of the theatre, of reading, of art and of nature. His father's sister, Mary, a widow, shared some of this experience with him; together they roamed the moors, spotting new plants, trees, birds. His own mother, Eliza, was severely loving, and apt to condemn his leisure pursuits as 'artistic'. His father Robert was an amiable sot, very much second-in-command in the household and in the hotel which they ran. Essentially, Laughton felt isolated within the family. When he married Elsa Lanchester, in his late twenties, they had planned to have children, but her discovery of his homosexuality put an end to that; it was, indeed, the first condition she laid down for the continuation of their marriage, and Lanchester reports that this was a great and continuing sadness for him. Laughton had warm, though unsentimental, feelings for children, and they liked him. The teaching which became so important to him from his forties on, was also, by extension, a form of parenting. Nurture was a crucial notion for him.

So there were many individual elements in *The Night of the Hunter* to which Laughton responded personally, quite apart from his love of the story-telling itself. That was paramount. He identified the form: 'it's a fairy-story, really a nightmarish sort of Mother Goose tale', he said, which immediately took it out of the realm of naturalism, let alone documentary realism of the type that Agee had attempted for his first draft. In their work together, he and Agee strove to find the essential story, stripping the narrative to its outline, condensing and contracting. They lost no characters, no scene, no location. They were unable to find an equivalent to the interior monologues. It is just possible that Agee, a master of that particular genre (*A Death in the Family* is filled with examples), attempted to introduce them into the film. In any event, if they were ever in, they went too.

In striving to find the language, the gesture, of the film with Agee, Laughton reran all of D. W. Griffith's movies at the Metropolitan Museum of Modern Art in New York with the writer at his side. In the January 1955 letter to Paul Gregory, Agee wrote 'I'm fascinated, and about 95% confident, in many of the things Charles learned and showed me out of the Griffith films we saw. If they do work, and I think they will, they're going to make the story-telling faster, and more genuinely movie, than they've been in many years.' This is what Laughton was trying to evolve: a narrative technique that was non-psychological and non-naturalistic, which combined visual expression with verbal rhythm, and this, essentially, is what they achieved in the screenplay published in Agee's posthumously published *Five Screenplays*. It is a shooting script, not a record of what was filmed, and there are a number of changes, and one crucial addition, which came later; these will be discussed in subsequent pages. (Even in those cases, it is now almost impossible to attribute direct authorship for the additions; Agee was often on the set and Laughton was very open to suggestion.)

The screenplay's most significant departures from the novel occur at the beginning and the end. The film – not the title sequence with Gish and the children; that is not to be found in the published text – starts with an incident not in the novel at all: the discovery by a group of children of the dead body of an old woman. There is a cut to the Preacher bowling along in his automobile, talking cheerfully to the Lord ('what is it to be, Lord? Another rich widow?'). The next cut takes us to a burlesque house where the Preacher is watching the show. We see for the first time the words tattooed on Preacher's fingers and watch his rising disgust till, finally, he presses the catch on the flick-knife concealed in the pockets of his jacket, and the blade rips orgasmically through the fabric. The police arrive, and apprehend him; he then appears in court, on charges of car theft. The screenplay then cuts back to another rural scene, where two children, John and Pearl, are playing with her doll. Their father, Ben, wounded, suddenly arrives in his car, with the stolen money, desperate to conceal it. He stuffs it into Pearl's doll, and makes John swear to look after it. Then the police – the blue men – arrive and take Ben away. He is tried and condemned to death. We cut to the house of the hangman, who, distressed by what he has to do, plans to give up his job. He steals into his own children's bedroom and stares fondly at their sleeping forms. We then cut to the jail, where Preacher and Ben Harper are sharing a cell. Harper resists his relentless interrogation over the whereabouts of the money. We cut to Ben Harper's execution; then to Preacher's release from jail. Thereafter, the narrative line of the novel resumes.

There are many good reasons why Laughton and Agee made the changes they did. They chose to start the film with Preacher to establish the presence of evil from the beginning and to avoid a later explanatory sequence in which Preacher's past and character would have to be revealed. The device of Preacher speaking directly to his Lord (the text lifted straight from the novel) sets up a certain stylisation of approach to alert us to the poetic idiom which will follow. The next decision, to play out the scene of Ben's arrest, is logical: the plot concerning the doll – that is to say, the *where's-the-money?* plot – is held back by Grubb, no doubt to increase the suspense, but in film terms, it is more suspenseful if we know just how close Preacher unknowingly comes to getting his hands on what he so ardently desires. Moreover, it puts us in the picture, so to speak, from the beginning: it gives us the primal scene, which is the driving motive of the plot – the oath John swears to his father. The loss is that John, whose story *The Night of the Hunter* is if it is anyone's, is not at the centre of events until some way into the film. The scene of Preacher's apprehension is a brilliantly effective piece of story-telling. The visit to a burlesque house is directly out of the novel ('he would pay his money and go into a burlesque show and sit in the front row watching it all and rub the knife in his pocket with sweating fingers') but the orgasmic penetration of the cloth, swiftly followed by the arrival of the police, makes for a brilliantly economical piece of story-telling. (A minor detail from the novel, omitted for reasons of time, is Icey Spoon's attempt to evoke the name of Willa's future spouse by consulting the Ouija board.) The other great change from novel to screenplay is in the final sequence, which has the same effect as the changes to the beginning: namely, that the story does not end with John. It has not been his story. The film simply ends with Rachel Cooper's (somewhat unproven) reassurance that the children will abide. The final shot is of Rachel's cosily snowbound house: a comforting end, but not, as in the novel, a conclusive one. Closure has not necessarily been achieved.

Almost all the dialogue in the screenplay is a variant on something in the novel; very often it is verbatim, or slightly tempered to mollify the censor (Lillian Gish is *not* accused of being the Whore of Babylon). There are two very striking lines, however, that have no origin in the book. Partly because of the performance of Lillian Gish, and partly because of their place in the film, they have a powerful resonance. 'I've been bad', Ruby confesses, tearfully. 'You was looking for *love*, child, the only foolish way you knowed how,' Rachel tells Ruby. 'We all need love.' Whether it was Laughton or Agee who wrote these lines, we shall never know; but it was a happy day for the film when they did.

PRE-PRODUCTION

The Night of the Hunter was published in February 1953, to immediate acclaim: 'a brilliant novel', said the *New York Times* critic. 'Make no mistake about it, *The Night of the Hunter* is a thriller which commands one's frozen attention. It is also a work of beauty and power and astonishing verbal magic.' Other notices were equally enthusiastic. At a certain point in the spring of 1954, when the main work on the screenplay was completed, Laughton began to consult Grubb, visiting him in

Philadelphia. 'He was just out of another world. I've known people back home that are different from the mainstream of sidewalk society, as he was, but I never knew anyone quite like him.' They bought take-out turkey drumsticks; Laughton threw one over his shoulder. 'Broke me up. It was just for effect of course. It was like giving me his signature or something. I can't put into words what Laughton contributed to my life, because he started to contribute to my whole, apperceptive mass as a writer when I was nine or ten years old. So, we kind of worked together 'til the time when he first started to direct movies.' Laughton wanted Grubb's input on everything.

Discovering that he had studied art at Carnegie Tech, Laughton asked him for sketches of certain scenes which he then showed to his collaborators. 'My dear Dave, The pictures are a real success. People say Oh! Oh Yes of course! There would have been all sorts of battles fought, preventing people from pushing it into a really good-looking film.' He asks Grubb – an advertising man in Philadelphia! – if he has 'a pet set designer'. Concerning the scene of Willa's testimony he has questions to ask: would there be flowers? Might it be in a tent? 'Drawings please,' he says. '*Now*. The journey of the children. I feel this passage should have the river behind it, visually and musically. It will be a brute to shoot as it will need so many more shots to the minute than the dialogue scenes. Any ideas for varying attitudes of the children?' He asks for advice about the music and tells Grubb that for the part of Rachel Cooper he's thinking of Jane Darwell (from Ford's *The Grapes of Wrath*) and dismisses Ethel Barrymore ('rather Hudson than Ohio River'). 'Hope this kind of uncareful letter is going to be the right way to keep the channels open to each other,' he says. 'Want to know all you have thought of, the best and the worst.'

Grubb's reply – a long (four page), tightly-typed screed – is illuminating at many levels. He suggests that there is something hysterical in Ben's desire to provide for his wife and kids when his job is 'a good one for those hard times'. Willa's obsession with the money once he's in jail is another manifestation of the 'economic neurosis of those times'. Sexually, Grubb feels, there is something furtive and guilt-laden about their relationship. 'What I'm trying to say is simply this: I do not believe that Willa and Ben's relationship was quite as emotionally and physically perfect as you seemed to feel.' This is a very suggestive remark in terms of Laughton himself. Grubb insists on the profundity of guilt in all sexual relations. Laughton was hardly a stranger to this idea, but wanted perhaps to counter it in his fable – to say that there *is* such a thing as guilt-free sensuality. 'No', says Grubb, 'The bud of guilt was there from the beginning for Preacher to bring so quickly into flower.' He then has a resonant phrase which must have stirred Laughton's old Catholic soul:

> Ecstasy slips so quickly from the loins to the praying hands … the whole Christian ethic is woven thusly – the gold thread of the spirit and the scarlet thread of the flesh … I simply do not think we can show Willa and Ben as pre-snake Adam and Eve without leaving unanswered the question: 'How could she endure such a man as Preacher if she had been so happy with a man like Ben?' Preacher you see brought Willa the punishment she had felt (perhaps since childhood) that she had deserved.

Whatever Laughton's view of sex without guilt, and the presence of this view in the film, the thread of poisoned sex which runs through the story is particularly well realised in the film.

Grubb is especially animated and enchanting about the sounds of the river. He knows a man, he says, Captain Billy, who knows that 'no film has ever had a true steamboat whistle in it. He knows that this sound cannot be made in a studio. He knows that it must be recorded after having drifted sweetly across living water as shoreside ears would hear it.' He recommends the sound of a calliope. 'It's a kind of holy, wonderful sound and I suspect it pries loose old pagan memories in the river-folk who may remember in their blood the pipes of the goat-footed men in the young grass at Stonehenge.' He offers daguerreotypes (from his Aunt Mary) of the original Cresap's Landing houses and sends a record of 'The Wreck of Shenandoah' for the composer, Walter Schumann. 'Please, PLEASE no folksy mouth-harp concerti with full Hollywood Bowl orchestra behind them.' As for casting, he says of Rachel 'her whole life is crisis – toughness always. Toughness to cover the love and softness that if she kept it out in the open would spill out and spoil.' Of the flight down river: 'The passage down the river must be a blessed and lyric moment of dramatic relief. I want the audience to feel the river as the womb of safety – as the flowing breast of source.' He promises sketches – the ideal means of communication for Laughton who, interestingly, was not at ease with ideas; his great strength was with images and sensations. Grubb tells him 'I am re-reading Moholy-Nagy's great work *Vision in Motion*. Don't worry. I won't go arty or Max Reinhardt on you. This is old stuff, long ago absorbed. I just want to refresh. It will help me to get at what I *saw* when writing the book.' As if being *arty* would alienate Laughton! Grubb didn't yet know his man.

Finally, he tells him that he has just resigned his job in advertising to concentrate on the film and a second novel. He signs off in a way that would
have pleased Laughton: 'Tonight is warm and I am unhappy because it
brings back the scent of a woman I loved last spring who went away.'

All this was deeply nourishing for Laughton as he prepared for the
labour of filming. He was indeed pregnant with the project. His
engagement with it was deep and personal. It seemed to be an ideal
solution to the problem of what to do with his life. His career had had an
unusual trajectory. His late start at RADA (where for a brief year he
studied) was followed by a meteoric rise in the theatre. In a series of
extraordinary character roles, the odd-looking young man brought a
startling vividness to everything he did, transforming the generally
rather shoddy vehicles in which he appeared into sensational artistic
experiences. By 1931, at the age of thirty-two, he was a dominant figure
on the English stage. He had been acting professionally for exactly five
years. He was greeted with equal acclaim on Broadway when he appeared
there, and was swiftly swept up by Hollywood, where again, he created a
sensation with some quite extreme characterisations, among them his
Nero in *The Sign of the Cross* and Dr Moreau in *The Island of Lost Souls*.
He returned to England to make *The Private Lives of Henry VIII* and
then again to try his hand at the classical theatre in a season at the Old Vic
which was not accounted a great success for him personally. He returned
to Hollywood, where, after a series of complex and flamboyant
performances – Captain Bligh, Javert in *Les Misérables* and Ruggles the
butler – he was routinely described as the greatest actor in the world. He
went back again to Britain, founding a production company of his own,
Mayflower Films, with the German producer, Erich Pommer, formerly
head of Ufa in Berlin. Nothing they produced (including *Jamaica Inn*
and *St. Martins Lane*) was entirely satisfactory, and in 1939 he returned
to Hollywood to give the performance that was immediately hailed as the
climax of his career: Quasimodo in *The Hunchback of Notre Dame*. For
many reasons, it proved to be the last of his overwhelming creations.
Thereafter, his work as an actor was craftsmanlike rather than inspired;
he tended to lend his personality to ventures rather than aspire to creating
the sort of iconic, archetypal figures of his earlier years.

His passion was turned in a different direction. In his personal life,
he began to find satisfaction with a series of male lovers; professionally, he
started to direct and to tell stories – though he would not have made a distinction between the two activities. His public readings – from the Bible
and the miscellany he presented in *Charles Laughton, The Storyteller* –

gave him another lease of life; and the décorless, costume-less reading of *Don Juan in Hell*, which he directed and in which he also appeared, caused a sensation on Broadway. Stephen Vincent Benét's epic poem, *John Brown's Body*, an unlikely candidate for dramatisation, was woven by Laughton into a tapestry of speech and music that made a revolutionary contribution to the art of theatre. This new lease of life was largely due to Paul Gregory who, seeing Laughton read from the Bible on *The Ed Sullivan Show*, had instantly spotted the financial potential, and arranged and managed the extensive tours across the country that Laughton now embarked on. It was Gregory who suggested the idea of a Shavian reading (though his idea was the preface to *Back to Methuselah*, not *Don Juan*), and who decided that Laughton should direct a film. After a reading tour, said Gregory, 'he would just *fade*. I wanted to bring Charlie into focus as a top director and have him eventually quit performing. The performances were what was killing him.' Laughton put it differently. 'Acting in movies only used a tenth of my energy. The unused energy, as it always does, was churning inside me and turning me bad.' His career as a stage actor had been brilliant but unsustained: apart from anything else, he lacked vocal and physical stamina. His career as a movie actor had been blighted by the circumstances in which commercial films are made. He began to discover himself and the public again with the reading tours; and he began to find fulfilment as an artist with the stage productions. But film had been his first passion, from his earliest years, and now everything was pointing towards this new departure.

Mindful of the opportunity being offered him, he now started very carefully to gather around him the team with whom he would bring forth the film.

THE CAST

Who would play Preacher? In a sense, the spell-binding evil man might, twenty years earlier, have been a Laughton part. His first instinct was a curious one: Gary Cooper. Laughton hugely admired Cooper, whose naturalness and ease eluded him, in life and art. It is hard to imagine Cooper bringing genuine terror to the role; in any event, he turned it down, feeling – no doubt rightly – that it would destroy his public image. Instead, at his prompting, Gregory claims, Laughton approached Robert Mitchum. 'Mitchum,' he told him, 'I'm directing this film and there's a character in it who is a diabolical shit.' 'Present,' replied Mitchum.

Mitchum was thirty-five at the time, veteran of an enormous number of films, for one of which – *GI Joe* in 1945 – he had received an Academy nomination as Best Supporting Actor (his first part had been in *Hoppy Serves a Writ* in 1943). Over the years he had evolved a distinctive persona compounded of laconic fatalism and a certain sexual mystery. Agee described it as 'a projection of pessimistic intelligence'. Mitchum and Laughton had met each other on and off in Hollywood, and from the beginning there was a surprising rapport between them. Mitchum was not given to expansive public utterances – indeed, interviewing him was something of a monosyllabic nightmare, as the present writer can confirm – but it was clear that he regarded Laughton quite simply as a master. Elsa Lanchester reports him coming to supper in Curson Avenue: 'In his anxiety to seem intelligent about it, he talked all through dinner ... I never heard such a lot of words – big, long words, one after another.' She notes their rapport: 'they were kindred spirits, both what you call rebels, with no formal respect for formal religion or Hollywood society.' Perhaps the closet intellectual in Mitchum was allowed by Laughton to emerge. If so, it was strictly in private. In public, he maintained his image as hell-raiser and all-round bad boy. His conviction, four years earlier, for possession of marijuana, and his criminal associations revealed in the course of the trial, had firmly established him in the public mind as a figure of thrillingly dubious morals, and made him, from that point of view, ideal casting as the psychopathic preacher. His eagerness to play the part must have been enormously encouraging to Laughton; he was the only other bankable element in the film. There were limits to his time: he would have to start shooting another feature, *Not as a Stranger*, during his last week on *The Night of the Hunter*, but he made it clear at the time where his real loyalties lay.

The second crucial piece of casting was Rachel Cooper, the benevolent antipode to Preacher's evil. The description in the book is crystal clear: 'She was old and yet she was ageless – in the manner of such staunch country widows. Gaunt, plain-spoken and hard of arm, she could stand up to three of the toughest shrewdest cattle dealers in Pleasants County and get every penny she thought her hog was worth.' Here again Laughton had a number of thoughts. As we have seen, he was enthusiastic about Jane Darwell (Mrs Joad in *The Grapes of Wrath*, whose line 'Can't nobody lick us, pa. We're the people' had seemed to sum up the whole film). The answer came to Laughton when he was rerunning the Griffith films. The perfect incarnation of threatened innocence in so many of them, Lillian Gish had matured into an actress of power and authority. For Laughton,

Lillian Gish as Rachel Cooper

she had a special, personal significance: at the end of the First World War, in France, he had watched *Broken Blossoms* over and over again, and when, in 1962, he lay dying in a coma, he roused himself to say, as if it were the key to his existence: 'I fell in love with Lillian Gish.' She conveyed some essence for him of profound, unsentimental goodness, which is exactly what he needed for the part of Rachel Cooper. Gish – fifty-eight at the time – had worked somewhat fitfully since the coming of sound and after *Duel in the Sun*, that mad David Selznick farrago directed by, among others, Sternberg, Dieterle, and Selznick himself, had vowed that she would never do so again. But Laughton proved persuasive. 'It was a very fine story of the basic human equation, a story of the battle of good and evil. I thought I could help him, so I told Charles I certainly was interested in the part.' He had another committed recruit to his team.

For Willa Harper, he chose an actress with whom he had a warm personal relationship: Shelley Winters, one of his regular students at Curson Avenue. In her autobiography she describes the effect Laughton had had on her. She writes of her first class: 'There is no present or award I've received in my whole life comparable to that which was given to me that afternoon ... When the studios told me I was a hunk of meat, a blonde bombshell, he made me understand I was an artist and a human being and I could demand respect and dignity.' She continued to attend the classes even while she was shooting films on heavy schedules. Finally she was pulled up by the head of Paramount because of the tell-tale bags under her eyes. 'Not every love affair is as important as every other one,' he gently told her. She explained to him about Laughton's iambic pentameter classes: 'We don't get to do a lot of Shakespeare here in the Valley,' he replied,

Laughton and Shelley Winters

Billy Chapin and Sally Jane Bruce

dumb-founded, 'so you make sure you get a good night's sleep.' Laughton identified in Winters a quality of sensual vulnerability which he saw as central to Willa, a more positive quality for him, as we have seen, than for the author. She was thirty-two at the time, having started, like Mitchum, in 1943, and earned a certain amount of respect (including an Oscar nomination as Best Actress for *A Place in the Sun*) as well as a degree of dismissal, precisely for being, as she said, a blonde bombshell. Mitchum, for one, was sceptical of her abilities, and remained so throughout the film. No doubt he regarded her as pretentious, but it was her pretensions, or at any rate her aspirations, that had endeared her to Laughton in the first place. More commitment.

Almost equal in importance to the three principals was John, the story's hero. Laughton had strong ideas about how to work with children. When nine-year-old Billy Chapin, who had had a big Broadway success in the play *Three Wishes for Jamie*, went to meet Laughton, Paul Gregory took him to Laughton's house and allowed him to steer the car while Mrs Chapin followed in her own car. Once at Curson Avenue, according to 'C LAUGHTON: TOT TUTOR', a cheery little piece in the *Los Angeles Times*, 'Mr Laughton, instead of mixing his famous martinis, invited Billy for a dip in the pool. The boy swam attired in a pair of Mr Laughton's trunks, their ballooning being held in with a belt.' Laughton and Gregory scrupulously refrained from asking him what he thought of the part or what the boy had done before. 'They just wanted to get to know him as a natural boy,' reported Mrs Chapin. 'I've been in this business for seventeen years, and I've never come up against anything like that before.' Little Sally Jane Bruce was cast as his sister Pearl. The rest of the cast was of distinguished pedigree:

James Gleason brings a lifetime of acting experience to Uncle Birdie

Evelyn Varden, the original stage Ma Gibbs in Thornton Wilder's *Our Town*, and Don Beddoe, outstanding on film in *The Face behind the Mask*, were to be the Spoons, Icey and Walt. James Gleason, Oscar nominee for *Here Comes Mr. Jordan*, an actor-manager and writer of great distinction, whose proud boast was that he had been onstage since babyhood, having been carried on at the age of two months, would play Uncle BirdieSteptoe. And Peter Graves, who had worked with John Ford, was slated for the small but critical part of Ben Harper.

THE CREW

While the casting proceeded, the rest of the creative team was chosen with meticulous care. The all-important appointment was that of Director of Photography. Laughton only ever appears to have had one candidate in mind: Stanley Cortez. They had worked together five years earlier on the

rather murky Simenon adaptation *The Man on the Eiffel Tower*, in which Laughton had played Maigret and had his first taste of directing a film. The original director had been sacked, so Burgess Meredith took over, ceding to Franchot Tone for scenes that he was in himself. When both were in a scene, Laughton directed. Stanley Cortez had arrived rather late in the day to solve problems with the Ansco colour system in which the film was shot. 'So you're taking the picture over,' said Laughton to Cortez on the latter's first day. 'Well, I'm happy to meet you, you big bastard.' To which Cortez replied: 'I'm very happy to meet you, you fat son of a bitch.'

As they began, so they continued; Laughton addressed the dandyish Cortez as 'the Brooklyn Spaniard' (though of course he was no such thing, having been born Krantz or Kranze). They had much in common: both were autodidacts, and neither was embarrassed by the word art. According to Cortez, after principal photography on the Simenon film was over and the rest of the crew had left Paris, he and Laughton worked happily alone together, shooting the city they both loved. (The footage is of no great distinction – though rather surprisingly Cortez won the Gold Award of the Société Française de l'Industrie Cinématographie for it. It certainly gives no hint either of the style they evolved for *The Night of the Hunter* or of the magisterial classical manner with which Cortez had supplied Welles for *The Magnificent Ambersons*.) They started from scratch on *The Night of the Hunter*, delighting in each other's company, going ever deeper into the poetry of film. 'There are only two people on the set, when it comes down to it,' said Cortez,

> the director and the cinematographer. Photographing *The Night of the Hunter* and the relationship that I had with Laughton was the most rewarding experience in my entire life and career, because of my love for this man, my great respect for him as a person and a great artist.

Laughton on set

Period. Charles and I had a rare, rare association, and a rapport that I'd never had with anyone before ... I knew what he was thinking and that what I was thinking coincided with this. Call it mental intercourse if you want.

Dreaming as a child of becoming an orchestral conductor, Cortez had started his film career as assistant to the great portrait photographer, Steichen. As a cameraman, he assisted Arthur Miller and Karl Struss; he worked extensively with the director Busby Berkeley. Early in his career he had made a 'cubistic' (his word) two-reel art movie which, characteristically, he called *Scherzo*. 'The subject-matter was, simply, water,' he told Charles Higham. He became head of photography at Universal Studios at the age of twenty-seven, where he carried on his experiments with a remarkable lack of interference. In *The Forgotten Woman*, he fondly recalled, he filled the screen with an eye 'so that you were looking through the eye as through a telescope into the recesses of the brain ... of course, people said I was much too arty.' Not Charles Laughton. The 'criminal slowness' of which Welles had accused him was for Laughton the ideal tempo with which to realise their dream. Before shooting commenced, Cortez went to Laughton's house where he met Agee. He brought a set of lenses with him to 'remind Laughton of what they were for', but by the end of the afternoon, Laughton was making Cortez think anew about their possibilities – not technically, but in terms of achieving the visual language that Laughton already had in his mind's eye.

Cortez was part of the movie-viewing sessions with Agee which also included the set designer, Hilyard Brown. They saw not only Griffith's work but also *Greed* and *The Four Horsemen of the Apocalypse*. 'Laughton,' Brown told Preston Neal Jones, 'really believed that pictures were motion pictures, not talking pictures.' Brown had worked on the subversively beautiful *Creature from the Black Lagoon* as well as assisting Perry Ferguson on *Citizen Kane*. To the team was added Robert Golden, the editor, who immediately saw that *The Night of the Hunter* was 'implanted in Laughton's mind, and he was a brilliant artist'. Finally, the composer, Walter Schumann, again the sole candidate for the job, was a figure of crucial importance. He had composed the inspired music for Laughton's stage production of *John Brown's Body*, creating a constantly varied choral tapestry of rhythms and sonorities. Though Laughton was not a musician himself, nor even especially attuned to music as such, he understood its function in both plays and films and had, in Schumann, found his ideal collaborator, familiar with the demands of theatre and television (he was the composer for *Dragnet*) and more than happy to participate in the whole process of filming.

In addition, Laughton hired the award-winning team of Terry and Denis Sanders as second-unit directors. Their documentary film *A Time Out of War* eventually won an Oscar. 'Brother Sanders!' he greeted the twenty-year-old Terry, fresh out of UCLA; 'Brother Laughton!' the young man cried back. He sat them down and drew precise, if spindly, line drawings of every shot he wanted, and that is what they shot, on location in Ohio: the helicopter shots of the river leading to the children's discovery of the murder victim in the first reel, and various shots along the river. It was not clear at the outset how much of the film would be shot on location, how much in the studio at Culver City, but the Sanders brothers were ready and eager for it, whatever it might be.

Gregory, as producer, despite his dynamic, even brash, personality was very happy to leave this team to get on with their work. He had faith in them, but even more important, he had faith in Laughton: 'well, if that fat son of a bitch doesn't know what he's doing', he said 'I'm dead anyway.' Everybody in any way connected with the film had that faith.

THE SHOOT

The atmosphere Laughton encouraged during the making of *The Night of the Hunter* was quite exceptional. A combination of total confidence in the material and extreme openness – not to say absolute trust – towards his collaborators created a mood of democratic commitment which is apparent in every frame of the film. Laughton was by no means an easy man, and had a widely-attested reputation, much promoted by Paul Gregory, for creating turmoil around him, but on this occasion – perhaps uniquely in his career – harmony was his watchword. 'The filming of *The Night of the Hunter*,' wrote Elsa Lanchester, 'was a compassionate time for Charles and he found that he was able to bring out the compassion in his performers.' The actors flourished under his gentle persuasion. It was not his way to impose specific readings on them: having cast them, he expected them to do of their best. Mitchum never ceased to regard Laughton as the best director he had ever had, though he had far cooler feelings for Gregory, which he demonstrated by urinating in the radiator of his car. His maverick behaviour continued unabated off the set: he and Shelley Winters were fond of sharing a drink when they weren't on camera, much to the disapproval of a woman sent from the

Welfare Department to protect the children. (Her protests ceased after Mitchum triumphantly discovered her swigging beer in a bush.)

But the rapport with Laughton while they were shooting was absolute. 'I knew what Charles was thinking, he knew what I was thinking. We had no problems, ever. I just tried to please him, you know, I was just showing off for him.' There was no discussion. 'As a director, he was so grateful, he went into ecstasy whenever he enjoyed the scene. He was adored.' Significantly, perhaps, in terms of their relationship, Mitchum adds: 'He was a sort of head of the family on the set, which is as it should be.' Laughton treated Mitchum with affectionate paternal indulgence, telling him, after the radiator incident: 'My boy, there are skeletons in all our closets. And most of us try to cover up these skeletons … my dear Bob, you drag forth the skeletons, you swing them in the air, in fact you brandish your skeletons. Now, Bob, you must stop brandishing your skeletons!' He constantly encouraged Mitchum to introduce a lighter note into his performance, a slightly slapstick quality. Half-humorously, he told Lillian Gish, who was confused by the dilution of evil that this entailed, that 'for Mitchum to play this all evil might be

Laughton with Gregory and actors from two of his stage productions bad for his future ... I'm not going to ruin that young man's career.' (This of the man who had only six years earlier been arrested and imprisoned for possession of drugs.) In fact, Laughton, with his strong sense of the absurd and his understanding of slapstick as a profound expression of the human condition, insisted on it to augment *The Night of the Hunter*'s fairytale quality.

Other cast-members were also vocal in their enthusiasm for Laughton's work. Lillian Gish said in an interview that 'I have to go back as far as D. W. Griffith to find a set so infused with purpose and harmony ... there was not ever a moment's doubt as to what we were doing or how we were doing it. To please Charles Laughton was our aim. We believed in and respected him. Totally.' He responded to her, in turn, with courtly graciousness. When Stanley Cortez unthinkingly referred to her in her presence as 'Gish', Laughton told her 'Stan uses the word Gish not to be impolite, but rather out of respect for you, as he would use the word Caruso, or Michelangelo – the great artists.' James Gleason – Uncle Birdie – said 'Charles is just terrific. He has a brand new way of handling people.' Peter Graves noted that when working for John Ford he had dared to say to the great director 'This part I'm playing: I think–', to which Ford had replied: 'Don't think in my picture.' 'Moving from Ford to Charles,' said Graves, 'was like walking from hell to heaven.'

Finally Laughton seems to have had a canny and successful relationship with the children: 'If rehearsal was necessary, it was effected when they were fresh – on the set, under the lights, just before each scene was to be shot' reported Helen Gould in the *Los Angeles Times*. 'Mr Laughton sat under a sound boom on the edge of the set, leaning over with round-shoul-

An unusual scene: Mitchum taking a director seriously

John holding out against
Preacher

dered intensity as though attempting to imbue each youngster with what
he wished through a sort of thought transference. "The knife, Billy," he
said to ten-year-old Billy Chapin. "There's danger in the knife! It cuts!
Sharp now, boy, a tight scene – like Mitch!'" (Chapin saw Mitchum as his
idol, and wanted, he said, to grow up like him.) Sally Jane Bruce, the five-
year-old playing Pearl, received his special attention: telling Billy how to
chase his sister, he shouted 'Go get her!' Then, says Gould, 'he followed
through with the action himself. He roughed the little girl up, then
enveloped her in a bear hug (not in the script!) before dropping her back
into the camera position on the rickety, dirty cot.' There were limits to his
patience however. Mitchum reported that he had one day, in Laughton's
hearing, given the boy an acting note, asking him: 'Do you think John's
frightened of the Preacher?' 'Nope' replied Billy. 'Then you don't know
the Preacher and you don't know John,' said Mitchum. 'Oh really?' said
Billy. 'That's probably why I just won the New York Critics' Circle prize.'
'Get that child away from me!', roared Laughton. But this was a rare
exception. The Cast and Crew photograph taken at the end of the shoot
shows Billy Chapin clutching Laughton's hand and roaring with laughter,
as is Sally Jane Bruce, held aloft in someone's arms.

Laughton's relationship with the crew was if anything even
warmer than the one he had with his actors. Of its nature, this
relationship was deeper and sustained over a longer time span. The pre-
production period was relatively short, but between them, the team
evolved a language for telling the film which was entirely consistent, and
strikingly original. Once shooting had begun, every night after the day's

work, Laughton would take his team – Cortez, Brown, Schumann, Golden, the first assistant director Milt Carter – for a meal at the Somerset Restaurant on La Cienega Boulevard. As they ate and drank they would plan the work of the day to come. To make himself clear, Laughton would sometimes read from Dickens, or ask Schumann to play some music. And he listened hard to what the team had to say. He had, said Brown, 'a kindly attitude to your ideas. Most people are not kind to ideas; they either accept them or they reject them. But he was not of that nature.' Golden was less enamoured of Laughton than were his fellow-collaborators – 'you might say I respected him but I didn't venerate him' – but he admitted that though 'he was demanding, he consumed you, it really was a lot of fun'. He created a democracy among his team – a rare phenomenon on a movie set, requiring a director of great confidence or exceptional humility. 'Laughton was never unsure at any time. There was never a man more sure of what he was doing. He didn't always do exactly what he said he was going to do because we all threw in our two cents' worth,' reported Hilly Brown. 'We all got mixed up in everyone else's business … Stanley Cortez was telling me how to do this, and I was suggesting to him how to do that, and we were all whispering ideas here and there in Laughton's ear. But in the end Laughton had the final judgement of how it was going to be done.'

Practically speaking, the day's shooting was very well prepared. Schumann would give an indication of the music for the scenes in question, Laughton would describe what it was that he wanted. Brown would sketch the elements of the set and make a rough story-board which the team would then discuss and modify; the final sketches were handed to Carter, who would hand them to the grips and electricians. This all proceeded like clockwork. 'It was designed from day to day in fullest detail,' said Cortez, 'so that the details seemed fresh, fresher than if we had done the whole thing in advance.'

From the beginning, Laughton had been insistent on conveying to all his collaborators the essentially fairytale-like quality of the story. Everything, he told Brown, should be seen from the boy's point of view. He accordingly designed the sets 'from the position that only children see certain things'. He and Laughton quickly developed an approach which consciously cultivated the use of simple means for evocative effect. The theatrical techniques of the Ufa film-makers were often borrowed, sometimes even quoted. There was little pretence that a real world was being filmed, the shapely lines and symbolic details creating a highly stylised environment in which expressive power was achieved by painterly or sculptural means, sometimes by quite explicit reference. They decided, for example, to shoot the church outing scene in the manner of Seurat's *La Grande Jatte*. They revelled in the chance to function as artists, not journeymen, and Laughton encouraged them at every turn. Their budget was not large, and they were confined to the studio, but they used their imagination in ways wholly appropriate to the fairy-story Laughton wanted to tell. The sense of improvisation, the creative moment, is strongly present in the finished film, what Brecht called 'the active creative element, the making of art', and what Truffaut, meant in his review of the film by 'an experimental cinema that truly experiments, and a cinema of discovery that, in fact, discovers'.

The famous underwater scene, for example, in which Willa's dead body is seen trapped in Ben's old Ford, with its willow roots rippling hauntingly in the river's strong flow, was shot in a tank on the set, the roots created by an upended fig tree hand-held by Brown himself, while electric fans dimpled the water's surface. The spider's web on the riverbank, through which the runaway children in their scull are glimpsed, was made of nylon thread on to which Brown dripped honey from a little stick to make dew. The walls in the A-frame room of such curious proportions in which Willa meets her death are made of muslin; the whole room is a self-contained little structure built on a platform, ten feet in front of which the actors played the scene. Most famously of all, the distant shot of Preacher, horsebacked on the horizon, was created by using Billy Chapin's double, a midget, on top of a donkey. The barn in which the children are sleeping and the farmhouse nearby are obviously cut-outs, while the stars above them are clearly dozens of small bulbs. Not for a second does this detract from the poetic intensity of the scene; but by some paradox the theatricality – and to all intents and purposes the scene is played on a stage set – is intensely cinematic, beyond mere photography, creation, not re-creation. It invites the imaginative collaboration of the audience, achieving what Laughton had told Lillian Gish was his ambition for the film, his lesson from Griffith: 'When I first went to the movies they sat in their seats straight and leaned forward. Now they slump down, with their heads back or eat candy and popcorn. I want them to sit up straight again.'

Despite the importance of Brown in creating the look of the film, it was, inevitably, Cortez who was Laughton's closest collaborator. He was particularly sensitive to the director's vision, translating Laughton's intuitions into technical reality. 'He would say to me, "Stan, this is where we need fantasy, this is where we need so-and-so and so-and-so ..." and

Hilyard Brown drips honey
onto nylon thread

Brown's A-frame: a stage
set that is intensely
cinematic

Billy Chapin's double, a
midget, crosses the studio
horizon on a pony

then he'd walk away and leave me alone and I would get these effects.'
Laughton had remarked on the fairytale quality of the journey down
river. 'When he saw the rushes, he said, "My god, how did you do that?"
and I said, "because you used the word fairy-tale."' Laughton proposed
to Cortez that the film should be shot in stark contrasts (despite Cortez's
initial impression that the film should have been shot in colour). He
started to experiment with Tri-X film, then very new, to Laughton's
perfect satisfaction: they were able to shoot scenes illuminated by no
more than a single candle. Cortez entered fully into the Griffithian world
that Laughton prescribed for part of the film, gleefully irising down the
lens (a device he had used to striking effect in *The Magnificent
Ambersons*) for the sequence when Preacher comes to find the children in
the house, keeping in mind Laughton's observation that Griffith
characteristically returned to the establishing shot of a scene at its end.
Equally, working with very few lights of great intensity, throwing
startling shadows across faces and surfaces, he entered with relish into the
German expressionist style with which the American pastoral manner
alternates in the film, a dialectical interplay of styles – night and day –
which is such a large part of *The Night of the Hunter*'s originality.

Above all there was a playful, passionate bond between the two
men, an absolute lack of self-consciousness about what they were
attempting to do. Cortez was excited by Laughton's concept of what he
called 'the dramaturgy of the film'. Of the last scene in the movie, with
Gish and the children, Laughton had said: 'This is like wrapping up a
Christmas scene, with a fancy ribbon, and that's it, ladies and gentlemen,
boom,' which to Cortez immediately suggested the Scherzo from
Mendelssohn's incidental music to *A Midsummer Night's Dream*, feather-
light, airy, spritely; and that is how he shot it. Cortez constantly thought
musically. When he was lighting the murder scene, Laughton had
demanded to know what he was thinking of. '"None of your goddam
business, Laughton," I said with great respect – we were like a couple of
kids he and I.' Finally he admitted that he was thinking of a piece of
music – Sibelius's *Valse Triste*. 'This was my key, and the given problem,
which only I in my own psyche was aware of. Now, to express this to
anybody but Laughton, they'd think, well, "Cortez is out of his mind,"
you know, "he's a long-haired phony," or "arty kind of a guy".' Instead
Laughton called for Walter Schumann and told him what Cortez had
said, 'and for the first time in my career, a man who wrote the music saw
what I was doing visually in that particular sequence so that he could
interpret it musically'.

Willa's trance-like
acceptance of death

Schumann was unusually present for a film composer. He was rarely away from the set, conceiving the musical sequences as he watched the scenes being filmed, constantly discussing them with the director. Laughton made clear to him the scenes where his music would be of paramount importance. 'In these scenes,' Laughton told him, 'you are the right hand and I am the left.' In shooting them Laughton purposely shot much more than the usual footage. 'This of course,' says Schumann, 'is a composer's dream; to have flexibility and not be tied to exact timing.' Laughton also drew Schumann's attention to a crucial principle: 'if the actors and I have stated it properly on the screen, then you don't have to re-state it with music.' He accorded the composer immense respect, to the extent that Bob Golden (who was also, somewhat reluctantly, in constant attendance on the set, having been banned by Laughton from the editing room) described Schumann as 'absolutely, next to Laughton, the most important contributor to the picture'. The film was thus the result of the input of almost all of the creative team, almost all of the time. This, too, is quite uncommon. Laughton insisted on Golden's presence because he needed his help, but also because he wished to supervise the editing himself frame by frame. A democrat he may have been, but he was also a leader. There was never any question but that the finished film would be his, which enabled him to be perfectly open to suggestion. Terry Sanders recalls his simplicity on the set, consulting, appreciating. 'He spoke very quietly, but you sure listened. He made you feel you were important, and *this* was important.' Golden recounts how, shooting the scene in which Preacher nearly stumbles upon Pearl playing with the hundred dollar bills stuffed in the doll, Laughton reached an impasse. He simply didn't know

47

what to do next. 'The one thing Laughton couldn't do was wing it. He didn't have the experience.' Suddenly – like Captain Bligh, as Golden says – he roared out 'Golden! What do I do now?' And Golden suggested the children's subjective reaction shot of Preacher, seen from below, one of the film's most striking moments. The affectionate cartoon signed by the cast and crew at the end of shooting shows, under the heading 'WE NEVER HAD IT SO GOOD', a number of images from the film dominated by Laughton's large mug on either side of which are the words 'WHAT THE HELL DO I DO NOW?' and 'I'M CONFUSED'.

Milt Carter made sure that the organisation was always flexible and efficient, maintaining the rhythm of the shoot, so there was a constant sense of forward movement. Nonetheless they slipped slightly behind schedule, which proved hugely to the film's benefit, because scenes like the children's drift downriver were shot in the studio ('when I tell people that, they go white,' said Cortez) rather than on location. By the end of the shoot, however, Mitchum was already hard at work on *Not as a Stranger*, also for United Artists, and his final scenes – the scenes of Preacher's arrest by the blue men – were completed on a couple of Sundays, at which the actor characteristically insisted on absinthe Suissesse being served to cast and crew. Whether because of the alcoholic consumption or for other reasons, they didn't get everything they needed; in the end Golden had to patch the scene together from what they had managed to film.

A parting gift to Laughton from cast and crew

In general, however, the shoot – accomplished in a nifty thirty-six days – had been highly satisfactory, including the Sanders' location work (interestingly, the only sequence they shot which was discarded was a shot of Preacher on horseback; its disappointing literalism led to the magnificent improvisation of the barnyard sequence). Even such a small job as the make-up on the dummy of Willa in the underwater sequence was in the hands of no less an artist than Maurice Seiderman, Welles's discovery, responsible for both *Citizen Kane* and *The Magnificent Ambersons*. Such was their delight with the rushes, that halfway through filming Laughton and Gregory had awarded percentages in the film to Golden, Brown, Cortez and Carter. There could scarcely be any clearer testimony to the positive and collaborative spirit of the shoot.

POST-PRODUCTION

The post-production period is above all in the hands of the editor and the composer. Both had been intimately involved in the shooting, so there was little doubt about the gesture that Laughton intended: the only question was how to realise it. Schumann was ideally placed to achieve his contribution: he had the footage, and in the editing suite he would sit with his piano, working out his thematic progressions and the textures he sought. He and Laughton were constantly concerned with meaning: how would the music tell the story. 'I could not use "Everlasting Arms" as underscoring for the Preacher,' he wrote, 'since this would dignify and create sympathy for his psychopathic religious beliefs. Therefore for Preacher I wrote what I considered a pagan motif, consisting of clashing fifths in the lower register.' Applying Laughton's principle of the contrapuntal use of music in relation to the scene, he created a deliciously sinuous waltz for the ghastly union of Preacher and Willa, which then plays through her murder and subsequent immersion in the Ohio river. Rising to the inspired realisation by Cortez and Brown of the children's drift upriver, he provided a passage of nature music among the loveliest ever written for film, music of freshness and benevolence, exquisitely orchestrated by Arthur Morton with an instrumental palette – replete with burbling, chattering woodwinds and flowing strings – strongly reminiscent of Honegger's *Pastorale d'été*. It is, in effect, as Schumann himself said, a twelve-minute tone poem, skilfully interweaving the themes of the two songs he had composed before shooting began, the exquisitely consolatory 'Lullaby' (to which Davis Grubb had written the words 'Dream, my little one, Dream / Though the hunter in the night/ Fills your childish heart with fright/ Fear is only a dream/ So dream, little one, dream') and 'Pretty Fly', sung by Pearl on the river: 'Once a time there was a pretty fly/ He had a pretty wife this pretty fly/ But one day she flew away, flew away./ They had two pretty children/ And one night the two pretty children/ Flew Away, flew away/ Into the sky – into the moon.'

Laughton had suggested at the outset that the composition should be accomplished in what he called 'long muscles': substantial unifying sequences. The final large section of this kind was created for Rachel Cooper, what they called the 'Hens and Chicks' theme, developed by Schumann into a scherzo-like movement. In addition, the unaccompanied songs that feature in the novel are perfectly placed within the overall structure of the film: the children's catch, 'Hing, Hang, Hung'; the harvesting round, 'Bringing in the Sheaves'; and above all Preacher's 'Leaning on the Everlasting Arms', sweetly and sincerely sung by Mitchum, another of Laughton's superb counterpoints. Sally Jane Bruce as Pearl had to be dubbed by Betty Benson (who had been one of the singers in Laughton and Schumann's *John Brown's Body*) while the lullaby is sung by the rich-voiced jazz-singer Kitty White, a possibly regrettable choice, causing the film to spill over into one of its very occasional Walt-Disneyish moments, offering routine glutinous sentimentality instead of the newly minted freshness of invention elsewhere. All in all, though, the score must be regarded as an absolute triumph without which the film would be an infinitely lesser achievement. But that is exactly how it was planned, from the beginning, to no less a degree than Bernard Herrmann's collaborations with Hitchcock and Welles or Prokofiev's with Eisenstein.

Golden in effect cut the film to the score. For the most part, this was no problem, since, as we have seen, Laughton overshot to accommodate just this process. The shot sequences in general had been very carefully designed by Cortez and were largely incorporated as conceived. Golden's real problem was the occasional lack of coverage due to Mitchum's departure from the film. On neither of his pick-up days were they able to shoot as much as they needed, so the editor was compelled to juggle what he little he had. The scene of Preacher arriving at Rachel Cooper's house, where he spots the doll, was a particular case in point. Golden, not a boastful man (he contemptuously dismisses the notion of 'cutters making pictures'), nonetheless states that whatever values that scene may have in the finished film 'were cutting values'. He provides a vignette of working with Laughton, by whom, as we know, he was not entirely besotted. He had been warned by his friend Hugo Fregonese of Laughton's charm, but had found it quite possible to resist it. Calling him 'a bugger to work with', he was extraordinarily taxed by the director's relentless demands in this testing sequence. Finally he threw his arms in the air crying, 'Charles, I can't satisfy you!' Laughton asked him to step outside the editing room, and they both sat down. Laughton said 'Bob, I want you to realise … I'm here … as your guest.' Back they went and finished the sequence.

There is very little by way of a sound score in the film since the music has such a controlling function. The recording of the voices is sometimes idiosyncratic, to some extent stylised, like every other aspect of the film. Voices which should come from afar seem close. Generally the sound picture is very much in the forefront, and it is hard to know whether this was conscious or due to technological limitations. It scarcely distracts from the film, but the impression is that this element was not accorded equal importance (as it is in the films of Welles, for example).

There is no doubt that the final film was exactly what Laughton wanted it to be – again, to extend the Wellesian parallel, as *Citizen Kane* had been for Welles (unlike virtually every other film in his output). Each member of the team had an opinion about separate sequences which they might have liked to have been different. Grubb was never comfortable with the element of slapstick that Laughton introduced into the scene in the cellar, for example, nor with the Ruby scene in New Economy. Golden believed that the lynching scene at the end should simply have been omitted (Grubb had his doubts about that too). Milt Carter believed that the opening sequence, from the discovery of Preacher's elderly victim by the children right through to his arrival at Cresap's Landing, was narratively unclear; and Gregory, incomprehensibly, believed that the classic river sequence would have been better had it been shot on location. He believed that the film was 'lost' from that moment on – the very moment when the film modulates into the poetry that for most people informs its most glorious sequences. Nonetheless, for all the collaborators, *The Night of the Hunter* was among their proudest achievements – and each member of this team had been central to the making of many remarkable films.

RECEPTION

The preview was not a success. It was already too late to change anything substantial, but Laughton had no desire to change anything. Much against the advice of Paul Gregory and many of the creative team, United Artists followed their usual saturation booking policy, simultaneously opening the film nationally and regionally. The reviews became all-important, and the reviews were complex. Not bad, by any means, as, in retrospect, they seemed to both Laughton and Gregory to be, but offering no clear view of the film. They were not, in a word, selling notices. But in most cases they engaged with both the nature of the material and the makers' treatment of it. The novel, of course, had been a sensational best-seller only two years before, and many of the reviews reveal at least a nodding acquaintance with it. This was partly as a result of what many might have regarded as a risky strategy on Gregory's part. In an article titled 'Reviewing the Bidding' in *Films in Review* which strikingly lays out the degree to which he wanted to break the hidebound approaches of the studios, he emphasised the need to cultivate critics, an underestimated part, he says, of the sales process. To that end he sent them all copies of the novel with the reviews. He then asks them for their opinions of the book. He speaks candidly of preconditioning, urging stop-overs in important towns. 'Hollywood producers,' he says, 'can build audiences through suitable and friendly contacts with local drama editors. He *is* the advance man. We ought to keep him out in front.' In another innovative and soon-to-be-standard approach, he sent stills '*without* the obvious suggestion that these stills were also suitable for newspaper reproduction'. How much of this plan he was able to put into effect is unclear; if he did follow it through, it could easily have been responsible for the slightly sniffy tone of some notices, using the novel as a stick to beat the film.

The other matters addressed were Laughton's direction, Mitchum's performance and the eternal conflict between so-called art and commercial values, a constant source of anxiety to American reviewers of the 1950s. Of the financially crucial reviews, Bosley Crowther in the *New York Times* was thoughtful but uncommitted: 'A weird and intriguing endeavor to put across something more in the way of a horror story involving children than the mere menace of the bogey-man is made in *The Night of the Hunter*,' he says, describing it as 'this audacious film'. He seizes on the phrase uttered by Lillian Gish about the children abiding as the film's central thesis, one, he says, 'difficult to render both forceful and profound in an hour and a half of tangled traffic with both melodramatic and allegorical forms'. He forgives Laughton for not bringing forth 'a wholly shattering picture', crediting him with 'a clever and exceptionally effective job of catching the ugliness and terror of certain small town types'. He believes the scene of the wedding night to be 'one of the most devastating of its sort since von Stroheim's *Greed*', but finds that 'the toughness of the grain of the story goes soft and porous toward the end' where 'the preacher pursuing, is the Devil; the little old lady is Goodness and Love'. Surprisingly he finds Gish 'sweet but whispy'.

The *Los Angeles Examiner*'s Dorothy Manners offers no such probing analysis: under the headline 'NEW LAUGHTON SCREENPLAY HAIR RAISER', she says, 'If it was Charles Laughton's intention to scare the scalps off the watchers of *The Night of the Hunter* ... he succeeded where this non-paying customer is concerned. Seldom has an entire production sustained the nightmarish feeling of helpless terror as does this picturisation of DG's symbolic novel.' Janet Graves in *Photoplay*, New York, echoed this, praising Mitchum as he was to be praised over and over again, generally in terms of ill-concealed amazement: 'In a suspense masterpiece, Robert Mitchum gives a performance of power and depth that nothing in his earlier career has even approached,' she says, adding that 'Charles Laughton uses the camera with the greatest imagination.' In the New York *Herald Tribune*, William Zinsser writes:

> Mitchum, whose acting has perhaps never been praised before, gives a superb performance that will surprise almost everybody. This is a tense melodrama brilliantly directed by Charles Laughton. On a deeper plane, it's a somber study of good and evil with characters more complex than the usual Hollywood type. On any plane, it's fine entertainment and one of the best movies of the year. Laughton ... has used close-ups to peer into the minds of his characters and he has filled the film with country noises ... sometimes Laughton gets too arty for his own good but *The Night of the Hunter* has so much imagination that we can forgive these excesses.

The *Los Angeles Times* spoke of it (approvingly) as 'one of the year's most unusual pictures'. Even David Bongard of the *Los Angeles Herald and Express*, finding it 'a curious picture' which 'certainly makes a bid for the "art" class of film, but in so doing some scenes are so giddily keyed that the dividing line between conviction and burlesque is disturbingly blurred', claims that 'had the opposing forces been less submerged in black and white affectation, it could have been a really great movie. It almost succeeds.' The words 'art' and 'arty', even when used approvingly, cut no ice with the broader market, and to praise a film by saying that it's out of the usual Hollywood mould, does it no favours – certainly not in the 50s of Eisenhower's America. At heart the problem of the reviews is that nobody seemed to know what kind of a picture it was.

There were certain violently antagonistic reviews. The *Washington DC News* was blunt: 'Robert Mitchum is not at all right ... somehow the gentleness and slow moral uplifting of all the characters is lost under the directorial hand of Charles Laughton ... the picture simply doesn't come off.' *Variety*'s Gene found that 'the relentless terror of Davis Grubb's story got away from Paul Gregory and Charles Laughton in their translation of *The Night of the Hunter*. This first start for PG as producer and CL as director is rich in promise of things to come but the completed product, bewitching at times, loses sustained drive via too many off-beat touches that have a misty effect.' In a hard-nosed analysis of its commercial chances he writes 'cast and credits will help the sale, and the genuinely different nature of the picture is probably a plus. Initial draw should be OK but the long distance b.o. staying power looks dubious for the general market.' Gene (whoever he might have been) denounces the 'pictorial lace', reckoning that 'the camera flourishes interfered with what may have been a competent script'. The New York *Film Daily* was dubious about its prospects too: 'filled with symbolisms, this initial Paul Gregory production appears best destined for special situations rather than general release. Its appeal lies in its unusual arty temperament, which should, of course, go well with certain groups ... screen treatment, which seems badly edited, was written by the late James Agee. Charles Laughton's direction, though creditable, seems overly dramatic in places, even tending to the farcical. This is carried over into the performances of Robert Mitchum and Shelley Winters.'

It would certainly have been possible to extract enough excellent quotes for Laughton, Mitchum, Shelley Winters, Lillian Gish and the film itself and to deploy them effectively in an imaginative selling campaign. But United Artists had no appetite for the task. The other film Mitchum was shooting for them, the lack-lustre *Not as a Stranger*, directed by Stanley Kramer, seemed to them a better bet, and so they shifted all their energies into promoting that. The chosen slogan for *The Night of the Hunter* does little to convey the particular quality and specific appeal of the film: 'The wedding night, the anticipation, the kiss, the knife, BUT ABOVE ALL THE SUSPENSE.' The image of a very glamorous looking Mitchum embracing an unhappy Shelley Winters, the hand with 'LOVE' tattooed on it across her back, the one marked 'HATE' clasping a knife at the level of her waist, is not entirely inappropriate to certain aspects of the film, but it omits the all-important presence of the children. On the level of a sexy murder story, the film fails: some awareness of the fairytale which everyone connected with the film was trying to tell should surely have be part of any promotion. In Britain, the film received an 'X' Certificate, so the whole aspect of the film as a child's nightmare had to be dropped. The trailer described the film as 'TOWERING ABOVE THEM ALL IN INTENSE EXCITEMENT', and made surprising reference to the team's theatrical provenance: 'The combined creative powers of Paul Gregory and Charles Laughton who brought *The Caine Mutiny Trial* to Broadway – now the screen receives the same electrifying impact.' The marketing was so feeble and so misjudged that Gregory wrote bitterly to United Artists suggesting that they might like to change their name to United *Against* Artists.

There were attempts to promote the film through other media: for RCA, on a long-playing record, Laughton recorded a condensation of the novel, written by Grubb, and spoken against a continuous collage woven out of the musical soundtrack (including Mitchum singing 'Leaning'). Laughton's rumbling delivery is low-key and almost off-hand but curiously effective. It's the kind of one-off notion which might have been successful had the film done well; instead it quickly became a collector's item but never a best-seller. In addition, Gregory somehow contrived a guest appearance for Winters and Mitchum on the massively popular *Ed Sullivan Show*, sponsored by Ford, from whom Winters demanded and got a blue Mercury as her fee. The programme was something of a disaster for the film. Neither actor was used to live television. Winters was hysterical, Mitchum drunk. He was almost inaudible, so the technicians turned up his microphone with the result that 'millions of viewers across the U.S. could hear our stomachs rumble', Winters relates. 'They were' she says, 'frozen with fear.' Mitchum held up the 'HATE' hand when he spoke of 'LOVE', which caused the studio audience to scream with laughter. Laughton was not best pleased that 'after all his careful direction we couldn't repeat for the live television cameras what we had already done on film'. The triumph of his work on the film was to have rendered material that might have been corny or crude subtle and poetic, while the nationwide extract from it – all that most people would ever see of it – reversed the process.

The film slowly ground to a standstill around America. Things were briefly enlivened by a ban imposed on the movie by an eighty-eight-year-old censor in Memphis, Tennessee, Lloyd T. Binford, who claimed that it was the 'rawest he'd ever seen', then cheerfully admitted that, like most of the rest of the movie-going public of America, he had not actually clapped eyes on it. It fared little better in Europe, being judged alternately lurid and quaint.

AFTERMATH

Even before filming on *The Night of the Hunter* had begun, Paul
Gregory, convinced that he had identified the *métier* in which Laughton
would flourish, had acquired a second property for him to direct:
Norman Mailer's brutally realistic Second World War novel, *The
Naked and the Dead*. He had heard Laughton talk about war and the
pity that war brought, based on his grim experiences in the trenches
during the last year of the First World War, and believed that Laughton
would again illuminate and transform the basic material. As soon as
The Night of the Hunter was completed, Laughton set to work on the
adaptation, retaining some of his team – Cortez, who started to do
preliminary reconnaissances, and the Sanders brothers, with whom he
worked on the camera script. With Agee dead, and his confidence in his
own powers as a writer finally established, Laughton took it on himself
to write the screenplay. Then *The Night of the Hunter* appeared, and
Laughton took its failure hard. He continued to work on *The Naked
and the Dead*, but according to Terry Sanders, his heart was not in it; or,
to say the same thing in another way, he had ceased to believe that it
would ever really happen, although Norman Mailer was powerfully
impressed by Laughton's contribution. A screenplay which he finally
produced was at least as long as Agee's initial draft for *The Night of the
Hunter*. Gregory had found a backer who asked for a costing, and when
this proved prohibitive, Laughton and Gregory fell out
comprehensively. Laughton had already been negotiating with a new
manager – perhaps on the time honoured principle that if things are not
going well in your career, a change of agent will solve everything – and
now the rift became formal and final. Gregory still had the rights in *The
Naked and the Dead*, which was eventually filmed under the
workmanlike direction of Raoul Walsh; despite tepid reviews, it
grossed, according to Gregory, 'millions and millions and millions'.
Laughton continued his reading tours under the new management of
Lloyd Wright (his and Gregory's mutual lawyer), and had something of
a return to the theatre, with an innovative *Major Barbara* in New York,
which he both directed and played in; a new play, *The Party*, in
London; and Bottom and Lear at Stratford-upon-Avon. The Bottom
was counted a triumph; the rest were found rather wanting. He made a
number of indifferent films in one of which – the bloated *Advise &
Consent* – he gave a devastatingly delicate performance of courteous
intolerance, while already stricken with the cancer of the spine which

was to kill him in 1962. His obituaries made scant mention of *The Night of the Hunter*.

Paul Gregory continued his successful career as a producer, first on the stage with *The Marriage-Go-Round*, starring Charles Boyer and Claudette Colbert on Broadway, his biggest success. He then worked happily for some years on television at CBS. In the 1980s he expressed himself entirely satisfied with the way his life had gone since the split with Laughton, though he was unable to conceal the loss of excitement in his work once the partnership had ended. Lillian Gish was unequivocal in lamenting the loss of their partnership. As for Gish, Laughton felt nothing but warmth towards her: 'Dear Little Iron Butterfly,' he wrote at the end of filming, 'Even though I talked to you yesterday I feel compelled to write you a note to tell you further that I think you are the living end ... I am happy to have had another Gish experience, and as long as I shall live and be active I hope that my life, professionally as well as personally, shall have a lot of Gish in it.' She went on to make a number of movies in the last years of her life, but none of them had the distinction of *The Night of the Hunter*. Mitchum and Winters continued their careers much as they had before working with Laughton, both making a large number of films whose only conceivable purpose must have been pecuniary. Mitchum occasionally suspended his habitual professional cynicism to give a number of very interesting performances, though nothing with the complex fascination of his Preacher. The children both gave up acting shortly after, as did Gloria Castilo (Ruby). No one's career was substantially boosted by the film. Walter Schumann died shortly (1958) after his work on the film, a real loss to film music; with this, his first film, he immediately placed himself in the Bernard Herrmann league. Cortez went on to photograph a number of films before his retirement in 1980 at the age of 74. He was given one last chance to demonstrate his experimental genius in the film *Blue*, directed by Silvio Narizzano. As for Davis Grubb, he became a prolific novelist and short story writer; his next novel, *A Dream of Kings*, set in the Civil War, was also turned into a movie, starring James Stewart, but it was neither a commercial nor an artistic success. Subsequent novels, *The Watchman* and *Fools' Parade*, were never even attempted. He had just completed *Ancient Lights* when he died, in 1980.

It took some twenty years for the film to establish itself widely as a masterpiece, and thus to endow its creators and performers with some degree of belated or posthumous glory.

REPUTATION

From the beginning, in certain quarters there was appreciation of the film and its aspirations, its complex and many-layered material offering the opportunity to discover meanings in it which may not have occurred to any of the people involved in its making – may, indeed, have horrified them. It is no doubt the destiny of a film widely described as symbolist (though perhaps 'imagist' might be a more fitting term) to be interpreted. Leo Braudy, in his influential *The World in a Frame*, startlingly proposes that 'in essence *The Night of the Hunter* is a film about the need to reject sexuality before one grows up enough to be tempted', a view which would have endeared it, no doubt, to the religious Right, but is strange to contemplate in relationship to Charles Laughton, from the point of view both of his opinions and his life. 'The process of the film is basically from Mitchum to Gish, from morbid anti-sexuality to reasonable and moral anti-sexuality, from a violent Old Testament religion, to a calming New Testament religion … *The Night of the Hunter* is a parable about growing up that rejects growing up unless the problems – both private and public – can be avoided.' Entertainingly he postulates a symbolic battle fought out between the silent-star Gish and the 40s and 50s star Mitchum. In allowing her to triumph 'it seems to reject the world in which Mitchum's personality took shape and to return instead to an Eden of aesthetic innocence. Although made in 1955, its emphasis on the romance of the studio set, the safety and articulation of the enclosed world, seems remarkably archaic now, a dream made possible by its style.'

Intellectually pleasing though this reading is, it scarcely adheres to the specifics of the film itself. Is sex the central issue with John? Sex seems rather one confusion amongst many issuing from the adult world. John's essential question is whom to trust, whom to believe in. He plays out good guy/bad guy games on his shadow screen in his bedroom. Confusingly, the blue guys, the cops ('good guys') arrest his dad. The Preacher, another supposed 'good guy', is deeply suspect to John, though to no one else. As if to underline this point, the film's epigraph concerns wolves who come in sheep's clothing. Rachel Cooper is the first person he finds whom he can trust, and even then he takes his time deciding. Sex, moreover, is not entirely absent from Rachel's household: Ruby is bursting with it, as are all those other girls whose love-children Rachel has inherited. (This is made more of in the novel. It is also interesting to note that in the book, the children are of both sexes; in the movie they're all girls.) She extends no moral disapproval whatever to Ruby's transgressions, although she has little patience with her continued infatuation with Preacher. Braudy's point about the nostalgia implicit in the shooting style is a telling one: in a sense Laughton, that most complex of men, seems to be aching for an older, simpler, Victorian set of values, both aesthetically and morally. The crux of the film, however, is *forgiveness*. John feels he's done something wrong; Rachel tells him he hasn't. The theological point about New Testament versus Old is curiously misplaced. Rachel's religion is improvised, interwoven with her life and that of the children. What she has made of it is more remarkable than what it is. Moreover, it's the *Old* Testament that she's reading from.

Truffaut, on the film's appearance in France, offered it a very warm welcome, while not being entirely convinced, calling it 'a bizarre adventure' and 'a cruel farce'. He detected 'failures of style' – 'the production flounders between the Scandinavian and the German styles, touching expressionism, but forgetting to keep on Griffith's track' – though he admired its inventiveness. 'It's like a horrifying news item,' he states, in a brilliantly suggestive phrase, 'retold by small children.' 'Screenplays such as this are not the way to launch your career as a Hollywood director. The film runs counter to the rules of commercialism,' he writes, adding with chilling accuracy, 'It will probably be Laughton's single experience as a director.' French writers in general have greatly admired *The Night of the Hunter*, perceptively locating it within the fantasy genre (le cinéma fantastique): Gérard Lenne regards it as containing its essence. He identifies Harry Powell as

> at once Croquemitaine, the bogey-man, terrifying with his magnified shadow, Blue-Beard marrying and killing all the young widows in the area, the Ogre sitting down to an enormous meal, frightening the starving Tom Thumb. Rachel Cooper is the Good Witch, the protecting Fairy, and her home, welcoming lost children, is like the Seven Dwarves' home, peaceful and hard-working. The flight down the silent river, the dark forest and its spells, all come together to create the atmosphere, anguished and alluring, of hocus-pocus, bad spells and nightmares.

In *Cahiers du Cinéma*, J. Goimard is eloquent about the way in which the studio-shot river with its starry, starry night 'derives from theatre décor and lighting; it is shown from the point of view of a child's gaze. We're in the world of wonders.' But he goes further; much further. He conceives the film as a family romance, telling the story from the perspective of a child's experience of the world, and particularly his experience of his parents. 'Why,' Goimard asks, 'do this father and this mother who only moments before were so adorable, now fill him with loathing? A hypothesis forms in the child's mind: they're not the same people – they've been switched with someone else.' Goimard notes what he describes as the diabolic doubling of Preacher for the father and the angelic substitution of Rachel for the mother. 'The female characters,' says Goimard, 'are not what they seem to be: behind the Oedipal problem is an even older and more terrible one. Isolated and in despair, John looks for a more effective protectress: first the river, so maternal that it holds the mother's corpse, whose hair is intertwined with its bindweed; then old Rachel, a real catcher of lost children. When Preacher is arrested by the police, John sees his father's arrest all over again; for the second time he loses this person with whom he refuses to identify, but who has made it possible for him to escape the embrace of an envious mother figure.' Like Braudy, Goimard fears a life of sexless bachelorhood for John. 'The little boy will stay committed to a world of cakes and affectionate admonishments. He will never become a man. No doubt about it, these Americans are always going to be big children.' Charles Tatum Jr, under the heading of 'The Evil Double of Charles Laughton', sweeps all this aside with a much more colourful suggestion. Not unreasonably, he suggests a parallel between Laughton and Preacher – both men who make a living reading from the Bible while nurturing unspeakable lusts.

Mitchum as fairy-tale ogre

Preacher, says Tatum, is the only character in the film who is truly alive, and he gets John, the object of his quest, at the very end, for a brief moment. While scudding down the wilder shores of interpretation, there is a certain suggestiveness about this notion that is not unilluminating.

Paul Hammond, in an article mysteriously entitled 'Melmoth in Norman Rockwell Land', rehashes the French critics' Freudian analyses and adds: 'Powell's fatal attraction to widows – "Well, now, Lord, what's it to be, another widow?" – is an indication of his own Oedipal compulsion' and extrapolates their theories about John's castration: 'indifferent now to Oedipal yearning, John, one can comfortably predict, will, in such anodyne, pious company, become a Walt Spoon.' It's hard to know why: he's a very attractive boy, and sex is omnipresent. Hammond then lurches into Marxist and aesthetic analysis: the film depicts 'the alienated relation of the sexes and the break-up of the family under capitalism … although the river and Old Mother Goose seem to offer an avenue of escape, the bleakness is unremitting, every couple's relationship is open to question.' This is to ignore, or at very least, to reject the film's unqualified uplift at the end.

British commentators have seized on the film's stylistic contrasts in a couple of very judicious pieces: Richard Combs in *The Listener* wrote that Laughton works through

> beguiling shifts of style, an eclecticism that puzzled reviewers at the time but which fits perfectly with a pantheistic sense of awe and wonder, a world where the boundaries between the natural and the unnatural, the sinister and the sublime, are fluid to say the least. It's part of Laughton's great sophistication and irony, blending contrary elements of the cinema itself: the kind of bucolic romance associated with the silent cinema, America as the Arcadian paradise of D. W. Griffith, combined with all the shadows that can be thrown by German expressionist lighting.

Writing of the film in the same journal some years later, a critic identified only as 'GM' says of the river sequence:

> something about this sequence remains elusively unique: although it recalls Thoreau and Whitman and even the American film documentarists of the 30s, there is an even stronger European lyricism about it, for its source seems to be pantheist and even pagan. It's an extraordinary moment in the American cinema, one of those rich

conjunctions of culture – the American pastoral, the European pantheist – which, if Laughton had been spared, or Hollywood had had the sense, he might have had a chance to give us another taste of.

A less conventional critic, Billy Wilder, who idolised Laughton as an actor, was unenthusiastic about *The Night of the Hunter*: 'he tried to put too much into it. Some things were very good – but with a first film you should never start with something big. I started with a neat little commercial film – quite funny, but nothing special.' The idea of Charles Laughton making such a film is almost hilarious in its incongruity. The French critic Robert Benayoun may perhaps be allowed the last word: 'To make only one film, but to make it a work of genius: isn't that, in the context of a journeyman profession, the shining example that Laughton has given us?'

CODA: A VIEW

The Night of the Hunter's triumphs of poetic cinematography and, as Laughton would say, dramaturgy, are well established. The acknowledgment of the work's achievement as a whole, despite the very occasional dissenting voice, is universal, and we have seen something of how it came about. I should like to end the book with a few personal observations on both form and content in the work. They are based on the conviction that most art is the outcome of human decisions and interactions, rather than the more sublime machinations of the sub- and super-conscious favoured, particularly, by the French school of criticism.

Laughton decided to frame his film (it may be assumed that it was Laughton's decision, since the shot does not appear in Agee's published screenplay) with an image of Lillian Gish as Rachel Cooper, surrounded by beaming-faced children apparently suspended in a stellar mid-heaven, as she reads them a text which discourages them from judging unless they be judged, and then warns them against wolves in sheep's clothing. Behind her sings a heavenly chorus: 'Dream, Little One, Dream.' Then Walter Schumann's pagan fifths crash out and we are plunged into the real world in a long helicopter shot over the Ohio valley which culminates in the camera's discovery of a dead body from which it pulls back, as if recoiling in horror. The barn in which the body has been thrown is surrounded by children, who abruptly stop singing their catch: 'Hing, Hang, Hung.' It is no disrespect to the film or its makers to say that this opening, in both its stages – the title sequence in the stars, and the discovery of the corpse – is a clumsy and confusing start to the film, both narratively and in tone. The visual and musical sentimentality of the title sequence is of the order of a mass-produced Christmas card (to which visual world, interestingly, the film returns at the end). The inclusion of Gish in the image (perhaps for commercial reasons – her appearance is otherwise delayed until over halfway through the film) anticipates the possibility of redemption. When she finally arrives the outcome of the struggle with Mitchum is never in question. Her untarnishable image must prevail. This of course is one of the reasons why Laughton finally cast her; but introducing her at the beginning of the film has an unbalancing effect on the film's journey. The other purpose of the title sequence is to introduce the notion of the dream, and indeed the Night of the Hunter ('Though the hunter in the night/ Fills your childish heart with fright/ Fear is only a dream'), but this, too, is clumsily done.

We are next introduced to the figure of Preacher, bowling along in his jalopy, an old Essex, in jaunty conversation with the Lord, against back-projected footage shot by the Sanders which looks exactly like what it is. The text is drawn from Preacher's inner monologues in the book, in which his warped mental processes are exposed at length. Here the effect is confusing. We don't quite understand the character, and don't necessarily associate him with the anyway deeply unconvincing dead body we've just glimpsed. Laughton knew as much; in a memo to Agee, he expressed his

doubts. 'It's too bad but I'm damned if I know how else to do it.' Mitchum, so centred and assured in the rest of the movie, does not seem comfortable at all. The sequence does, however, have a unique tone, both theatrical and stylised, and it paves the way for the wholly original language Cortez and Laughton evolved to tell the rest of the story. This visual idiom is revealed in the very next sequence, when Preacher goes to a strip show. The economy of the scene-setting is striking, but there is no attempt at naturalism.

Distilled imagery

Preacher's arrest

(Curiously, Mitchum, so supportive of the film and Laughton's vision, later opined that he believed that this scene would have been much better shot on location.) The background figures, like puppets, streaked with shadows, are silhouetted in front of a brightly lit wall, which can have no counterpart in reality. It's simply a crystallised image, a painting, almost, of a certain situation, with Preacher similarly abstractly lit in the foreground. We are given only the visual information we require: the girl Preacher is watching, his hands tattooed 'LOVE' and 'HATE', the knife ripping phallically through the material of his jacket, the policemen, finally the policeman's apprehending hand on his shoulder.

By now, the film has hit its stride and barely falters. The scene in the court, the second overhead shot with John and Pearl and their father, Ben Harper's arrest – in that strangely graceful staging which Laughton felt appropriate to the scene which haunts John through the

Ben Harper's arrest

book, though not the film – the scene in prison with Preacher and Ben Harper, which precisely reproduces Preacher's swinging down the bunk as described in the novel and which introduces us to the use of diagonal framings and slanted angles which Brown, Cortez and Laughton were to repeat so often and so powerfully throughout the film. The effect is always one of expressive intensification, demanding the audience's heightened awareness. Well partnered by Peter Graves (an exceptionally handsome man of the open, masculine sort to whom Laughton was so attracted sexually), Mitchum in the course of the scene gives us almost the whole gamut of his performance: wheedling, hortatory, cynical, sincere. Does he believe what he says, or does he not? Impossible to say. The performance is almost two-dimensional; both the actor and the character seem to be giving conscious performances, which lends a highly original dimension. At the risk of introducing an over-used and devalued tag, this is a Brechtian performance in the technical sense of the word – it is a demonstration of a certain kind of behaviour which promotes an analytical and critical attitude from the audience. It might be said that it is Preacher who is giving the Brechtian performance, not Mitchum. Character becomes a

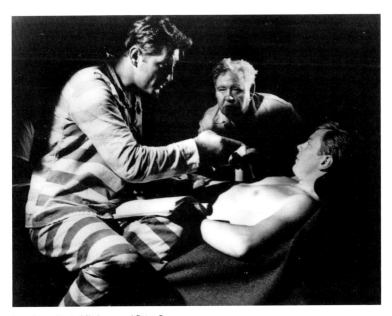

Laughton directs Mitchum and Peter Graves

kind of conjuring trick: the fascination comes from watching the way in which Preacher works his effects. The more naked the contradictions, the more chilling the effect. It is not exactly Grubb's Powell, the Preacher of the book, who is a more familiar evangelical character, not a seducer and a charmer like Mitchum's. It may not be fanciful to compare Mitchum's Preacher with Molière's feigning priest, Tartuffe, who equally flaunts his behaviour in the sublime confidence that he has hooked his victims to the degree that he only needs to offer token nods in the direction of credibility. Ben Harper resists Preacher but we have no doubts that there will be no giving up on Preacher's quest for the money. Ben meanwhile goes to the gallows with some dignity – in another cleanly economical shorthand sequence – having kept his secret.

The sequence in which the hangman returns to his family after despatching Ben is a skilfully condensed version of what Grubb wrote in the novel, and introduces the note of compassion and social justice – the Fritz Lang element that the French critic notes – which echoes through the film. 'Hing, Hang, Hung' sung over the sleeping bodies of the hangman's own children is a typical instance of expressive compression. The Griffithian pastoral mode is well established in the depiction of Cresap's Landing, to be shattered by Preacher's arrival by train – another slanted angle, another phallic thrust. When thinking of the film in its historical context it is hard to banish thoughts of another hunter, equally complex and oddly persuasive, who stalked the land of America, causing fear and anxiety in, amongst others, Charles Laughton and Robert Mitchum. The comfort and somnolence of the Eisenhower period had been shattered by the activities of the junior senator from Wisconsin, Joseph McCarthy. While Laughton and Agee were writing the screenplay, in 1954, his reign of terror was coming to an end but its legacy was everywhere. He too had come with a sword to bring destruction on the enemies of the Lord. It is not suggested that Laughton and Agee – nor indeed Grubb – were making a conscious parallel, but there is a striking resonance. America had just come through a nightmare; bogey-men were by no means the preserve of children's literature.

The sequence of Preacher's arrival outside Willa's house is again a very close reproduction of what Grubb originally wrote, though the shadows themselves are quite unrealistic (John's shadow could scarcely be as big as Preacher's), as is the sound. Preacher's seductive chant of 'The Everlasting Arms' is quite artificially loud, as if in the room, or in John's head. The sense of the child's point of view comes and goes: it is by no means systematic. In fact, every time it happens, we are pulled up short, reminded of the child's perspective, with a consequently heightened sense of danger. Our first glimpse of Shelley Winters' Willa is in the ice-cream parlour where she works for Icey and Walt Spoon. The sense of sexual innuendo in the air, and Winters' palpable sense of unfulfilled desire is strongly suggested. Evelyn Varden as Icey gives a wonderful impression (if admittedly on the theatrical side) of the dramas of small-town life. Grubb said of her: 'She put things into that characterisation that she should have got *extra* for. She should have been made a member of the corporation.' The sense of Willa's passivity is enhanced by Varden's dangerous interfering energy. We understand that Preacher is entering territory in which the fruit is ripe for picking.

The team's desire for visual distinction sometimes operates independently of meaning: in an early shot of Uncle Birdie on his boat, singing to his own guitar accompaniment, the camera peers at him through an upturned scull, while the water creates patterns of light which play on his face; it is a very attractive shot, but not a meaningful one. Very occasionally there is a sense of straining for this sort of effect; this is partly what the first critics meant by the word 'arty'. Even Paul Gregory said in an interview with Preston Neal Jones, 'There can be *too much* art direction.' Sometimes, too, the creation of an interesting frame is done purely visually, without much attention being paid to the action within it. When John comes back

from Uncle Birdie to discover Preacher holding Willa, Pearl and the Spoons rapt with his fable of love and hate, the scene – supremely well played by Mitchum – is curiously static, both in the placing of the actors – lined up against a wall – and in camera movement, which is negligible. On occasion, it seems, Laughton has determined that certain scenes are plot scenes, or perhaps that they will look after themselves, but the contrast with the intensely cinematic realisation of other sequences is too great: they simply seem dull and lack-

Preacher's fable of love and hate

ing in dynamism from a filmic point of view, well though they are played. It may be said without too much generalisation that the day sequences are somewhat less inspired cinematically than the night ones, both interior and exterior, for the obvious reason that night offers the greater opportunity for use of light and shadow, which Cortez exploits to the full, though the picnic sequence, with its dappled light and the startlingly low camera angle for Mitchum's first attempt to get John to tell him where the money is, the *Grand Jatte* sequence, is menacingly beautiful.

The wedding sequence is given wonderful lift by Schumann's waltz; there is some sort of family feeling between it and the waltz Bernard Herrmann composed for *The Magnificent Ambersons*, with a similarly unifying effect. The scene in the hotel – Willa's second wedding night – is brilliantly staged and designed, and given a force that was not in the novel by the casting of Mitchum, whose virility and relative youth make Willa's dashed expectations the more intense. In fact, the relationship between Winters and Mitchum is altogether more highly charged than that of the characters in the novel; there is an element of sexual torture in them, of arousal denied, that adds powerfully to their scenes together. The subsequent revival meeting, again achieved by theatrical short hand – simply

The picnic sequence modelled on Seurat's *La Grande Jatte*

Willa's second wedding night

Preacher forces Willa to reject her natural
desires

Willa denounces her former life

69

Expressionism meets the
mid-West

created by two flambards and a handful of extras – achieves more than any literal staging might have managed. The famous murder scene is quite startlingly unrealistic, a highly self-conscious composition set in a room of no graspable geography, and self-consciously acted. But it succeeds triumphantly in its integration of setting, lighting, music and performance,

Mitchum's skull tilted towards the light like a death's head as he waits for his instructions from above, Winters awaiting her inevitable death like a child receiving its first communion. The scene in which Preacher brings the news of Willa's disappearance to the Spoons is the high point of his Tartuffe-style: nakedly false lamentation, so bold as to suspend disbelief. The juxta- position of this with Birdie's discovery of the body in the water, and his subsequent descent into drunken paranoia, as he addresses his dead wife in her photo frame, builds the tension as the threat

to the children grows. The justly admired interlude of Willa's submerged body, in which the wedding waltz has become distant and full of far-away harmonics, is irradiated with Cortez's powerful lights, their beams coming from no observable or logical source. It is a scene of transfiguration, an almost mystical scene of quite exceptional power.

When the knot begins to tighten on the children, we see Preacher from behind approaching the house. We can just see two little faces at a window near the ground; as Preacher passes them by the camera irises down onto the faces. So begins the controversial section of the film in which Laughton deliberately tilted the sequence in which Preacher is at his most dangerous and ruthless towards comedy. With a variety of means – including constructing an unreally small cellar to emphasise Preacher's great size in relation to the children – John and Pearl's desperate evasion of their step-father is given a *Tom and Jerry* dimension: Preacher is humiliated and outwitted. The danger is never wholly suspended – Mitchum always carries an edge of danger with him, however the situation may be stacked against him – but the film is very much on the side of the children and administers a series of thwacks over the head, including collapsing shelves and treacherous staircases, to the homicidal Preacher. Mitchum perfectly colludes with a style of performance which would not be out of place in a Keystone Cops movie (it is worth remembering that Laughton, without any sense of artistic slumming, had recently acted in *Abbott and Costello Meet Captain Kidd*).

This section of the film, up to and including the children's last-minute escape down river, leaving Preacher up to his waist in water, howling with animal rage, deeply disturbed Davis Grubb; it bore no relation, he felt, to what he had written. He claimed that every time the sequence started, he averted his eyes from the screen. In later years,

The Tom and Jerry sequence in the cellar

though, he acknowledged that Laughton had been right in the context of the film. It was a necessary transition to what followed, the flight downriver, for which Grubb (who had always seen the river – the river he grew up on – as central to the story) shared the general admiration. Laughton, Schumann and Cortez's conception of this sequence is of a healing by nature; the 'Lullaby' becomes central to it. The poetic transformation begins almost immediately. A series of shots from different angles of the boat with the children on board takes us away from the feverishly subjective mood of what precedes it; the magical appearance in the foreground of the shot of various creatures – egret, frog, turtle, rabbits – creates a feeling of extraordinary natural benevolence. Interspersed with these sequences are the scenes in which Pearl and John try to beg for food from the local farmers. For these scenes, Cortez creates a grainy feeling resembling the great Walker Evans photographs of the Depression in the South (accompanying Agee's *Let Us Now Praise Famous Men* as it happens); perhaps there were more of these scenes in Agee's original draft. As it is they are harsh interludes in what remains an essentially idyllic transition in the film, counterpointed with Preacher's unrelenting pursuit of them.

'The boat began moving, blessedly moving, spinning at first like a mad October leaf'

John and Pearl give
themselves over to the river
and nature's healing

The scene in the barn is purely visionary, something worthy of a Samuel Palmer; at the same time, it is deeply theatrical. There is no pretence whatever that we are anywhere other than in a film studio, and we are invited to appreciate the aesthetic effect. Again, Cortez's imagination creates exquisite images: when Pearl and John enter the barn, the scene is shot from below, through the cow's full udders. When the nightmare intrudes here – with the distant sound of Preacher crooning 'Leaning, leaning' and his appearance on the horizon – it is of a piece with the dream-like quality of the whole section. John, in close-up with a deep-focus background, wearily asks 'Don't he ever sleep?' With the appearance of Gish's Rachel Cooper, briskly ordering the children about to the musical accompaniment of her plucky 'Hens and Chicks' theme, we know that they are safe. The film endorses her absolutely. In Gish's magnificent evocation of sturdy goodness, there is little of the novel's sense that she is a disappointed woman, rejected by her own son as being too much the old country woman to be part of his life in the city, and driven by frustrated maternal instinct to adopt waifs and strays, living in constant fear that the authorities or the families will reclaim them. No, Gish's Rachel is a transparently decent spinster, unsentimental, for the most part, but without complications. John and Pearl, we feel, have come home.

The switch of tone when the film follows Ruby to nearby New Economy is abrupt. We are in the Big Town and no mistake, garish, full of bright lights, neon and temptation. The sex that fills the air is credible and like nothing else we have seen so far in the film. Gloria Castilo's Ruby might almost be a young Willa, filled with unassuaged longings which the

Gloria Castilo's Ruby
ensnared by Preacher

boys leaning against the wall instantly pick up on – though Grubb again worried that this scene was inauthentic to the world that he knew and about which he was writing. Preacher's arrival on the scene and Ruby's immediate infatuation with him are swiftly effected; Mitchum skilfully suggests the sexual disgust behind his seduction of the nubile young woman. Back at Rachel's, the setting is again stylised as she relates the Pharaoh story to the children: the cut-out hills beyond the parlour window are artificially lit to create a frank tableau, an image. An atmosphere of serenity prevails. Gish is sturdily tender when she absolves Ruby for her flirtation with Preacher (needless to say, in the film the novel's revelation of her sexual encounters with the boys of New Economy is softened). Rachel offers love without condition and strength without threat; it is this that finally heals John's unhappiness and brings the nightmare to an end.

Preacher's arrival at Rachel's house is played with the light sense of slapstick – Powell finds himself staring down the barrels of a shotgun – that Laughton encouraged in these sequences. The night scene when Preacher takes up his vigil under the street lamp, in a near mirror-image of his first appearance outside the Harpers' house at the beginning of the film, uses a zoom lens to good effect, taking us inside and then outside without cutting. Again the imagery of the night is introduced to haunting effect, this time showing nature in a less benevolent light, as the owl sweeps down on the rabbit. 'It's a hard world for little things,' Rachel observes. When Preacher finally invades the house, Rachel fires on him, which sends him scuttling out of the house in good Mack Sennett manner, hooting and

Preacher arrives at Rachel Cooper's haven for abandoned children

hollering as he grabs the seat of his pants. We are in the dénouement now. Rachel calls for the police; they arrive the following morning, and we see the film's second arrest, consciously filmed to match the first. John can bear it no longer and throws the doll with dollars streaming out of it at the feet of Preacher; he, after his night in the barn, hardly registers it, any more than the police do. Neither in the novel or the film is there any resolution of the question of the money: what happens to it? The truth is that by now, the money, which has been the main engine of the plot, is insignificant, because John and Pearl are on their way to rehabilitation. John, in particular, has learned that money can never justify human suffering, of which he has experienced more than any child should.

The film cannot reproduce the novel's remarkable interior monologue for John in which his unconscious dissolves all the events of his past, including his father's arrest and the whole horror of Willa's death and the flight from the Preacher. Instead we have the court scene in which John refuses to testify, then the mob scene, in which the Spoons and their neighbours from Cresap's Landing have become vengeful Bacchantes, out for blood. This sequence is brilliantly realised (*pace* Robert Golden), with its haunting glimpses of the seemingly comatose Preacher in the police van and Ruby still desperate for the man she loves. It closes on the hangman's grim line 'this time it'll be a pleasure', which is effective enough but scarcely conveys the sense implied in the novel by Grubb's phrase 'Preacher's dreadful last night on earth', suggesting a Tennessee Williams-like (or Euripidean) act of bodily destruction. Through it all, Rachel in her Mother Goose mode marches the children back to her haven.

It is Christmas, and the children receive and give presents. John shyly brings Rachel an apple that he wraps in a serviette, and receives in exchange the watch that he has always craved. We end with the Christmas card image of Rachel's snow-covered house, which is a poor substitute for the novel's return of John to his shadow-filled bedroom and his understanding that the nightmare has finally ended.

It is harsh to accuse a film which has dared so much of not quite going the final lap. The achievement of Laughton and his team is exceptional and enduring, the imagery original and haunting, tapping into the subconscious and a world of fears and longings; the story-telling is assured and compelling. It was one of the first, pioneering independent productions, and it remains a fine example of a film which defies all formulas, as well as a supreme example of the integrated work of a team. Laughton's failure to make another film is a serious loss to the history of the movies, but his one masterpiece continues to inspire those who share his sense of the expressive possibilities of the medium.

Laughton surrounded by his cast and crew near the end of the happiest experience of his life   77

CREDITS

· ·

The Night of the Hunter

USA
1955

©1955 Paul Gregory
Productions
Production Company
Paul Gregory Productions
presents
Released thru United Artists
Produced by
Paul Gregory
Production Manager
Ruby Rosenberg
Directed by
Charles Laughton
[2nd Unit Director
Terry Sanders]
Assistant Director
Milton Carter
[Dialogue Director
Denis Sanders]
Screen Play by
James Agee
From the novel by Davis
Grubb
Photography by
Stanley Cortez
[2nd Unit Photography
Harold Wellman]
[Camera Operator
Bud Mautino]
[Camera Assistants
Seymour Hoffberg, Robert
B. Hauser]
[Gaffer
James Potevin]
**Special Photographic
Effects**
Jack Rabin, Louis De Witt
Film Editor
Robert Golden
Art Direction by
Hilyard Brown
Set Decoration
Al Spencer

Property Man
Joe La Bella
Wardrobe
Jerry Bos
[Wardrobe] Assisted by
Evelyn Carruth
Make-up
Don Cash
**[Make-up of Willa's
Corpse**
Maurice Seiderman]
Hairstylist
Kay Shea
Music by
Walter Schumann
[Orchestration
Arthur Morton]
Soundtrack
'Lullaby' performed by
Kitty White
'Pretty Fly' performed by
Betty Benson
Sound
Stanford Naughton

Cast
Robert Mitchum
Harry Powell
Shelley Winters
Willa Harper
Lillian Gish
Miss Rachel Cooper
James Gleason
Uncle Birdie
Evelyn Varden
Icey Spoon
Don Beddoe
Walter 'Walt' Spoon
Billy Chapin
John Harper
Sally Jane Bruce
Pearl Harper
Gloria Castilo
Ruby

[*uncredited*]
Paul Bryar
Bart, the hangman
Mary Ellen Clemons
Clary
Cheryl Callaway
Lary
Corey Allen
young boy in town

Black and White

8,139 feet
90 minutes

Credits checked by
Markku Salmi, BFI
Filmographic Unit.

The print of *The Night of
the Hunter* in the National
Film and Television Archive
was aquired specially for the
360 Classic Feature Films
Project from United Artists.

NOTE ON SOURCES

· ·

The Library of Congress in Washington has a substantial archive relating to *The Night of the Hunter* bequeathed by Elsa Lanchester; Madeleine Matz and her colleagues were miraculously efficient in lending me materials at the shortest possible notice. The greatest debt I owe is an overwhelming one. Preston Neal Jones has spent many years of his life compiling an oral history of the film, 'Heaven and Hell to Play With: The Filming of *The Night of the Hunter*', of which a condensation has appeared in Iris Newsom (ed.), *Performing Arts – Motion Pictures* (Washington, DC: The Library of Congress, 1998), pp. 52–99. The whole work, however, has never been published, which is a great loss to film history. Jones conducted lengthy interviews with all of the participants in the filming, the great majority of whom have since died; the resulting work, a skilful collage in which the interviewees tell the story of the making of the film in their own words, is an enthralling document on which, with the author's generous permission, I have drawn extensively.

In addition I have consulted the following texts.

Benayoun, Robert, *Dossiers du Cinéma* (Paris: Casterman, 1971)

Braudy, Leo, *The World in a Frame: What We See in Films* (Garden City, NY: Anchor Press/Doubleday, 1976)

Eels, George, *Robert Mitchum: A Biography* (London: Robson Books, 1984)

Combs, Richard, 'Night Flight', *The Listener*, vol. 115 no. 2950, 6 March 1986, pp. 28–29.

Goimard, J., 'La nuit du chasseur', *Avant-Scène* (special issue), no. 202, 15 February 1978, pp. 3–22.

Grubb, Davis, *The Night of the Hunter* (1st edn 1953; London: Prion, 1999)

Hammond, Paul, 'Melmoth in Norman Rockwell Land … on *The Night of the Hunter*', *Sight and Sound*, vol. 48 no. 2, Spring 1979, pp. 105–9.

Higham, Charles, *Charles Laughton: An Intimate Biography* (London: W.H. Allen, 1976)

——, *Hollywood Cameramen: Sources of Light* (1st edn 1970; London: Garland, 1986)

Lanchester, Elsa, *Elsa Lanchester Herself* (New York: St Martins Press, 1983)

Laune, Gérard, *Le Cinéma 'Fantastique' et ses mythologies* (Paris: Editions du Cerf, 1971)

Thomson, David, 'A Child's Demon', *Sight and Sound*, vol. 9 no. 4 (NS), April 1999, pp. 20–22

Truffaut, François, *The Films in My Life* (New York: Simon and Schuster, 1978)

Winters, Shelley, *Shelley, Also Known as Shirley* (New York: William Morrow, 1980)

——, *Shelley II: The Middle of My Century* (New York: Simon and Schuster, 1989)

Finally, I would like to thank Mr Peter Richards, of Bridgend. He will perhaps be surprised to find himself thus acknowledged, since he wrote a letter to *Sight and Sound* of breathtaking rudeness and arrogance in which he summarily dismissed the opinions about the authorship of the screenplay I expressed in my book *Charles Laughton: A Difficult Actor*. Spurred on by his scorn, I determined to investigate the matter in somewhat greater depth than I had originally done, and as a result I have revised my view to suggest a considerably more complex evolution of the screenplay. For this, I thank Mr Richards, of Bridgend, though I doubt whether my final conclusions will satisfy him any more than my original ones.

ALSO PUBLISHED

An Actor's Revenge
Ian Breakwell

L'Âge d'or
Paul Hammond

L'Année dernière à Marienbad
Jean-Louis Leutrat

Annie Hall
Peter Cowie

L'Atalante
Marina Warner

L'avventura
Geoffrey Nowell-Smith

Belle de Jour
Michael Wood

The Big Heat
Colin McArthur

The Big Sleep
David Thomson

The Birds
Camille Paglia

Blackmail
Tom Ryall

Bonnie and Clyde
Lester D. Friedman

Boudu Saved from Drowning
Richard Boston

Bride of Frankenstein
Alberto Manguel

Brief Encounter
Richard Dyer

Das Cabinet des Dr. Caligari
David Robinson

Cat People
Kim Newman

Chinatown
Michael Eaton

Citizen Kane
Laura Mulvey

Double Indemnity
Richard Schickel

Les Enfants du paradis
Jill Forbes

42nd Street
J. Hoberman

"Fires Were Started –"
Brian Winston

The Ghost and Mrs Muir
Frieda Grafe

Greed
Jonathan Rosenbaum

Gun Crazy
Jim Kitses

High Noon
Phillip Drummond

In a Lonely Place
Dana Polan

It's a Gift
Simon Louvish

The Life and Death of Colonel Blimp
A. L. Kennedy

Lolita
Richard Corliss

M
Anton Kaes

The Magnificent Ambersons
V. F. Perkins

A Matter of Life and Death
Ian Christie

Meet Me in St. Louis
Gerald Kaufman

Metropolis
Thomas Elsaesser

Napoléon
Nelly Kaplan

La Nuit américaine
Roger Crittenden

Odd Man Out
Dai Vaughan

Olympia
Taylor Downing

Palm Beach Story
John Pym

Pépé le Moko
Ginette Vincendeau

Performance
Colin MacCabe

Queen Christina
Marcia Landy & Amy Villarejo

Red River
Suzanne Liandrat-Guigues

Rocco and his Brothers
Sam Rohdie

Rome Open City
David Forgacs

Sanshô Dayû
Dudley Andrew & Carole Cavanaugh

The Searchers
Edward Buscombe

The Seventh Seal
Melvyn Bragg

Shane
Edward Countryman & Evonne von Heussen-Countryman

Singin' in the Rain
Peter Wollen

Stagecoach
Edward Buscombe

Sunrise – A Song of Two Humans
Lucy Fischer

Taxi Driver
Amy Taubin

Things to Come
Christopher Frayling

Went the Day Well?
Penelope Houston

Wild Strawberries
Philip & Kersti French

The Wizard of Oz
Salman Rushdie

If you would like further information about future BFI Film Classics or about other books on film, media and popular culture from BFI Publishing, please write to:

BFI Film Classics
BFI Publishing
21 Stephen Street
London W1P 2LN

BFI Film Classics '… could scarcely be improved upon … informative, intelligent, jargon-free companions.'
The Observer

Each book in the BFI Publishing Film Classics series honours a great film from the history of world cinema. With new titles published each year, the series is rapidly building into a collection representing some of the best writing on film. If you would like to receive further information about future Film Classics or about other books on film, media and popular culture from BFI Publishing, please fill in your name and address and return this card to the BFI.* (No stamp required if posted in the UK, Channel Islands, or Isle of Man.)

NAME

ADDRESS

POSTCODE

E-MAIL ADDRESS:

WHICH *BFI FILM CLASSIC* DID YOU BUY?

* In North America and Asia (except India),
please return your card to:
University of California Press, Web Department,
2120 Berkeley Way, Berkeley, CA 94720, USA

BFI Publishing
21 Stephen Street
FREEPOST 7
LONDON
W1E 4AN